A TASTE *of* TAIN

From the Highlands of Scotland

COURT HOUSE TOWER

Published by the

TAIN GALA ASSOCIATION

Taste of Tain
Compiled and Edited by Carole Herd

Art Design by Melissa Gray, Grayscotland Ltd. www.grayscotland.com

Taste of Tain published in 2005 by
Tain Gala Association
Sutherland House, Bank Street, Tain, Ross-shire Scotland IV19 1AQ

www.tain.org.uk

All photographs © Mike Herd
except for the carved church mouse © Richard Easson, food photographs
by the individual contributors concerned
and Mr. Carnegie's dining room from Skibo Castle.

Front cover and "this desirable premises" © Mike Taylor.

Pen and ink illustrations © Richard Easson © Lucy Ballantyne

Printed by
Posthouse Printing & Publishing Ltd,
Findhorn, Moray, Scotland www.posthouse.org

Tain Gala Association
cannot accept responsibility
for the authorship of contributors favourite recipes.

A TASTE *of* TAIN

FOREWORD BY
TAIN GALA ASSOCIATION

Tain Gala Association was formed in 1986 with a view to create and promote a good

mix of sporting, social and educational entertainment, for all age groups for one

week each year. For the past eighteen years they have endeavoured, not only to

run a successful Gala Week, but also to succeed in filling the gap on the social

calendar by introducing other events throughout the year as and

when appropriate.

The success of their activity in Tain can be measured by the support they receive

from local people resident in the 30 miles radius of the ancient and Royal Burgh,

as well as that of the visitors, and ex-patriots, who take their annual holidays to

coincide with Tain Gala.

Tain Gala Association is run by a voluntary committee. They are a fully constituted

body with office bearers and members appointed at their AGM. Regular meetings

are held to discuss the aims of the organization.

Alasdair Rhind,
Chairman
2005

ILLUSTRATION BY RICHARD EASSON

A TASTE *of* TAIN

INTRODUCTION

Situated 36 miles north of Inverness, in the beautiful north-east of the
Scottish Highlands, is the Royal Burgh of Tain.

The town has a long and fascinating history. The town's Gaelic name,
Baile Dubhthaich, means Duthac's town, and it is to St Duthac that the town owed its
early importance. By the late Middle Ages his shrine, in Tain, was established as one
of the most important pilgrimages in Scotland. Tain was granted its first
royal charter in 1066.

One of Scotland's oldest Royal Burghs, the 1066 charter, granted by King Malcolm III,
confirmed Tain both as a sanctuary, where people could claim the protection of the
church, and an 'immunity', whose resident merchants and traders were exempt from
certain types of taxes.

Throughout history Tain has played an active part in many dramatic and renowned
events. King James IV regularly made pilgrims to Tain to achieve both spiritual
and political aims; Robert the Bruce sent his family to Tain in 1306 to keep them safe
from the English; in 1745 the troops of Bonnie Prince Charlie spent time in Tain and
a century later the repercussions of the Highland clearances were being felt
in Tain's court-house.

Tain, and the nearby village of Inver, was hugely important to the war effort during
World War II, with secret D-Day landing exercises taking place on the local beaches.
Although this caused enormous disruption to the lives of the local people, they rose
to the challenge. A strong and independent spirit which still exists today.

Tain has a population of 3,500. Members of the community are passionate about their town, which is witnessed through the existence of a large number of voluntary groups who all work together to preserve and improve the beautiful environment, social and recreational facilities and ensure economic growth. Tain people enjoy coming together in celebration. During the summer months there is the annual Gala Week and the famous Glenmorangie Highland Games, which attract competitors from all over the world. Throughout the year Tain is host to regular market stalls, town fairs and street parties. These events are primarily led by the Tain Gala Association, a band of dedicated and enthusiastic volunteers. Celebrations are not complete without music and performances, and again Tain can boast of its talent and enthusiasm.

The traditional music group, Gizzen Briggs, not only hold regular events in Tain but have played throughout the world. Both young and old are members of the Garrick Singers, Tain's renowned choral group, who hold regular performances of light opera and oratorio. Scottish music is always in the fore through the regular performances of Tain's own pipe band.

When strolling throughout the town it is impossible not to stop and marvel at the many beautiful buildings, designed and built by many famous architects. The St Duthus Collegiate Church is recognised as one of the finest medieval buildings in Scotland and the Parish Church, Royal Hotel and museum are fine examples of the work of the famous architects, the Maitland family. All these buildings are now interspersed with a range of specialist shops, mostly family run businesses. Tain is as famous now as it was in history; it is recognised for its whisky, pottery, silver, fine cheeses and mussels.

Recreation plays an important role in the lives of many in Tain and the surrounding area. There are a great number of maintained and informal walks in and around Tain which take in the breathtaking scenery, wonderful wildlife and enable people to enjoy the crisp fresh air of this part of the world. Sport plays an important role through the Royal Burgh of Tain Golf Club and its fine links course, bowling at the local green, tennis at the all-weather floodlit courts and team sports on the recently completed all weather pitch. Young people in the area enjoy their own activities at the skate park, the play park, the outdoor football pitches and in their own Youth Cafe and drop-in centre.

A special feature of the town and its community is the bringing together of old and young. There are many activities which enable all generations to join together and share experiences and views. The Youth Cafe is a striking example of this.

Tain Youth Cafe is run by adult volunteers and provides a venue for over 100 young people from Tain and surrounding village communities to enjoy. Through community fundraising the young people were able to purchase their own building and stock it with computer technology and sporting equipment. The young people from the Cafe regularly host events and performances for all the community to enjoy and take an active part in all community events.

Tain is a wonderful mix of both traditional and modern. The community strive to ensure that Tain prospers as they develop modern facilities and attractions while as the same time continuing to embrace the traditional, historic features of the town which make Tain so special. Visitors and the community can step back in time when visiting Tain Through Time, set in the beautiful churchyard around St Duthus Collegiate Church. The museum and Pilgrimage run by the Tain and District Museum Trust explores the history of the Burgh from its earliest time. Tradition is also maintained in many of the businesses from bakers who use traditional ovens to make their bread to the famous Glenmorangie Whisky Distillery who create malt whisky using the same craftsmanship of their fathers and grandfathers. The modern world is also embraced with facilities such as all day nurseries, after school clubs and holiday play schemes for working families, clubs and societies for both old and young and a wonderful mix of shops from complimentary therapy clinics and beauty salons to traditional ironmongers.

Historically Tain was a haven, a place of Pilgrimage. This sense of history still prevails today. Enter Tain and you are transported back in time through the beautiful architecture and the many traditions that are still maintained. Tradition is also demonstrated through the warmth and friendliness of the people in Tain; this is a town where people take the time to stop and talk, where a friendly smile is always forthcoming. Recently a successful businessman in Tain was asked what brought him to Tain. He told a story of his very first visit to Tain, when during a morning stroll in to the town centre every person he passed that morning wished him a 'Good Morning'. Such hospitality and friendliness is an abiding image of Tain.

Alasdair Rhind
Chairman, Tain Gala Association

INDIVIDUAL RECIPES & CONTRIBUTERS

STARTERS

curried parsnip soup ~ *Carole Herd*
easy chicken soup ~ *Karen Livingstone*
hare soup ~ *Mrs Joyce Fraser*
hough soup ~ *Rae & David Robertson*
tony's smokie soup ~ *Tony Watson*
strathdon soup ~ *David Lauritsen*
bacon, prawn & cheese paté ~ *Carole Herd*
smoked mackerel paté ~ *Tanya Brooke*
chicken liver paté ~ *Cathy Shankland*
game paté with green peppercorns ~ *Prue Douglas-Menzies*
blewits & cream ~ *Jamie Stone (MSP)*
baked chicory ~ *Susannah Stone*
black pudding with blue cheese dressing ~ *Pat Gibson*
mussels cooked in oatmeal ~ *Roddy Robertson*
smoked salmon or trout tinbals ~ *Jean Paterson*
smoked salmon or trout savoury tartlets ~ *Prue Douglas-Menzies*

MAIN

roulade of beef with smoked salmon & hramsa in a red wine sauce ~
Graham Rooney, Head Chef, Delny House Hotel
balblair angus whisky pepper steak ~ *Lesley Whitlaw*
steaks with whisky cream sauce ~ *Alasdair Rhind*
steak & stilton ~ *Mandy Rhind*
steaks highland cattle beef cooked swedish style (tjaelknoe) ~ *Alan Torrance*
beef olives filled with haggis & creamy whisky sauce ~
Head Chef, St Duthus Hotel
beef cobbler ~ *Connie Beaton*
supper or lunch with left over haggis ~ *Hazell Gill*
chicken with whisky sauce ~ *Father Andrew & Imelda McMichael*
castlecraig chicken salad ~ *Liz Whiteford*
tasty crispy chicken ~ *Murray Macleod*
chicken broccoli bake ~ *Maggie McAuley*
chicken carol-land ~ *Lorraine Christy*
coachhouse chicken ~ *Iain Mackenzie*
chicken summer salad ~ *Tain Library*
wild boar terrine with apricots & prunes ~
David Graham, Head Chef, The Glenmorangie Highland Home at Cadboll
seared glenmorangie whisky and citrus marinated loin of roe deer ~
David Graham, Head Chef, Glenmorangie Highland Home at Cadboll
venison steaks with a port & orange sauce ~ *John Munro Butcher*
venison stew ~ *Mrs Hazell Gill*
duck breasts lemon with redcurrant jelly & port sauce ~ *Tony Watson*
ducks with grapes & herbs ~ *Prue Douglas-Menzies*
juicy pheasants with apples & calvados ~ *Prue Douglas-Menzies*
pheasant casserole ~ *Liz Mackenzie*
loin of lamb with chantrelle rosti ~ *Chris Driver, Head Chef, Skibo Castle*
taste of tain kebabs with ceilidh couscous ~ *Robert Hudson*
ragout of lamb with red wine ~ *Fiona Scott*
lamb & lentil chilli ~ *Lorna Macnab*
easter ross lamb with rosemary & onion sauce ~ *Mary Mackenzie*
stuffed pork tenderloin ~ *John Munro, Butcher*
loin of pork in white wine sauce ~ *Susannah Stone*
lemon pork chops ~ *Joannie Whiteford*
mussels in two sauces ~ *Frank Mahon*
mussels with sun dried tomatoes ~ *Frank Mahon*
stuffed mussels ~ *Frank Mahon*
lemon & garlic prawns ~ *Carole Herd*
fish casserole ~ *Pat Chilvers Steele*
uncle angus's fish pie ~ *Paul Moclair*
partan pie ~ seasoned crab soufflé ~ *Gordon Robertson, Oystercatcher Restaurant.*

grilled red mullet on a pea tomato risotto ~
David Graham: Head Chef, Glenmorangie Highland Home
scampi provençale ~ *Ross Bannerman*
fillet of balnagown sea trout filled with a hand-dived moray firth scallop
mouse-line ~ *Graham Rooney : Head Chef, Delny House*
seared fillet of sea bass with a pesto mash & a saffron & cream butter
essence ~ *Denis MacKay, Head Chef Mansfield Castle Hotel*
marinated tuna steaks ~ *Grace Williamson*
salmon patties ~ *Janet McKeachan*
salmon fish cakes with tartare sauce ~ *Trish Geddes*
salmon morangie ~ *Brian Campbell, Head Chef Morangie House Hotel*
dave's memorable salmon steaks ~ *David Macdonald*
grilled salmon ~ *Charles Brooke*
mike's marinated salmon ~ *Mike Herd*
stuffed pumpkin with cheese & white wine sauce ~ *Susannah Stone*
mediterranean pasta ~ *Lucy Ballantyne*
peasemeal pakora ~ *Ian Smith*
vegetable pasta ~ *Margaret Urquart*
vegetarian lasagne ~ *Fiona Robertson*

PUDDINGS

plate apple pie ~ *Mrs Edith Ross*
spiced pears ~ *Hazel Gill*
scottish fruit tart with whisky ~*Craig Eccleson*
monteagle raspberry pudding ~ *Mrs. Helen Jones*
gooseberry crumble ~ *Paul Moclair*
party pudding ~ *Connie Morrison*
lucy's wicked chocolate dessert ~ *Lucy Woodley*
traditional german cheesecake ~ *Neil Munro*
balblair elements raspberry cheesecake ~ *Lesley Whitelaw*
iced banana parfait ~ *David Graham*
frozen strawberry & zabaione terrine *David Graham*
tain summer pudding ~ *Melissa Gray*
old man schneider's five families tiramisu ~ *Paul Moclair*

BAKING

cranberry bread ~ *Tain Royal Academy Community Complex (TRACC)*
quick bread ~ *Melissa Gray*
nut bread ~ *Alasdair & Brenda Mearns*
special queencakes ~ *The Wool Shop*
ginger raisin cake ~ *Mrs Barbara Rae*
lemon curd fatless sponge ~ *Trish Geddes*
aunt mary's 'salami' ~ *Tranquillity Health and Beauty*
granny shivas's boiled fruit cake ~ *Muriel Watson*
chocolate yoghurt cake ~ *Richard Easson*
brambles carrot cake ~ *Christel Mercer*
iced 'porridge' (biscuits)~ *Rhoda Corsie*
flora's flapjacks ~ *Flora Stone*

MISCELLANEOUS

glenmorangie fizz ~ *Rachel Barrie*
farmhouse lemonade ~ *Paul Moclair*
elderflower champagne ~ *Susan Harding-Newman*
lassie sweet & sour yoghurt ~ *Paul Moclair*
date & apple chutney ~ *Carole Herd*
plum chutney ~ *Prue Douglas Menzies*
bannocks a pictish recipe ~ *Caroline Shepherd-Baron*
martin's favourite easy breakfast ~ *Martin Watssman*
ankerville house nursery baby unit porridge ~*Margaret Eunson*
children's mayonnaise ~ *Irene Dewing*
bacon~banana bombshells ~ *Mike Taylor*

CONTENTS

(for a more detailed list of all recipes and contributors see over)

ILLUSTRATION BY DAVE CHAPLIN

favourite recipes...

STARTERS

curried parsnip soup

serves 6   *Contributor:* **Carole Herd**

1½ oz butter

1 onion, skinned and chopped

1 tsp curry powder

2 pt chicken stock

3oz single cream

2 lb parsnips peeled and sliced

1 potato peeled and sliced

½ tsp ground cumin

salt and pepper

10 fl oz milk

Melt butter, add parsnip, onion and potato. Saute for 3 minutes

Stir in the curry powder and cumin. Cook for 2 minutes

Add stock, bring to the boil and simmer until vegetables are tender

Puree in blender until smooth

Reheat, adjust seasoning, add cream and milk

easy chicken soup

serves 4   *Contributor:* **Karen Livingstone**

1 medium skinless chicken fillet (cut into cubes)

1 teaspoon of olive oil

2 organic chicken stock cubes
(made into 750ml (1½ pints) stock

3 sliced leeks

2 tablespoons of fresh parsley

salt and pepper

Heat a large saucepan and put in olive oil, and chicken.

Cook for 5 minutes until meat is sealed.

Add chicken stock, sliced leeks and 1 tablespoon of parsley. Season, bring to the boil and simmer for 25 minutes.

Add more stock if needed.

Add remaining tablespoon of parsley just before serving.

Karen Livingstone, of Adorable Accessories, doesn't have much time for cooking! She enjoys making her beautiful designer bags suitable for both day and evening wear and if given half the chance would devote every minute of the day to this. She is also known for her very attractive hot water bottle covers which go like hot cakes during the cold North of Scotland winters. Her recipe is quick, easy and very sustaining, especially if served with hot crusty bread – just the thing for a middle of the day snack!

hare soup

serves 6

Contributor: **Mrs Joyce Fraser**

1 hare (full hare cut into joints by your butcher)

beef dripping for frying (lard or cooking oil can be substituted if preferred)

2 large onions, chopped

340g (¾ lb) chopped carrots.

340g (¾ lb) chopped turnip

2 teaspoons mixed spice

3 tablespoons plain flour

1½ pint beefstock

You can always be sure of a warm welcome and good hospitality at Joyce's house. Her Hare Soup was a big favourite at New Year by well wishers in need of sustenance before the walk home.

Brown the joints in a large pan, using beef dripping.

Add the chopped onions, carrots and turnips and stir thoroughly.

Cover well with beef stock or 2 beef stock cubes mixed with water - retaining a small quantity with which to make the roux).

Simmer gently until the meat is tender.

Remove the meat and keep aside to chop into bite sized pieces to serve along with the soup.

Liquidize the soup.

Mix the flour and mixed spice in a bowl and make into a roux with the retained stock.

Gradually stir into the soup and continue to stir until the soup thickens and the flour is thoroughly cooked.

Do not allow soup to boil.

Season.

Remove from the heat and serve in hot plates and allow the family to add the hare meat as they fancy it.

Note: Crusty bread is a good accompaniment. A pre-boiled 'Golden Wonder' potato can also be added to each plate of soup.

hough soup

serves 3-4

Contributor: **Rae & David Robertson**

½ cup pearl barley steeped in water overnight.

225 g (8oz) shin of beef - cubed

450g (1 lb) potatoes - peeled and diced

1 large onion - finely chopped

10g (½ oz) butter

salt and pepper

Melt butter and sauté the onion and set to one side.

Brown the cubed beef in the same saucepan as the onion.

Bring 2 pints salted water to the boil and add cubed beef.

Boil for 20 minutes and then allow to simmer for 15 minutes skimming the pot as necessary.

Bring back to the boil, add barley, potatoes and finally the onion and continue cooking for about 25 minutes.

Season to taste and add more water if mixture is too thick.

Serve with bread and butter.

Local chemist *David Robertson* is very knowledgeable about Tain's history and tells many a great story! However after hearing about his culinary skills in the kitchen involving a tin of cat food, it was decided that perhaps his wife Rae would be a better option for the Taste of Tain recipe!

tony's smokie soup

serves 6

Contributor: Tony Watson

1 arbroath smokie

3 potatoes, peeled and diced

1 large onion, chopped

1 leek, sliced and washed

sea-food cocktail

double cream

salt and pepper

Firstly, strip all flesh off Smokie.

Make stock with bones and skin and cook for 15 minutes.

Strain liquor into pan and add potato, leeks and onions and cook until tender.

Add fish and any sea-food (if liked) to pan and warm through for 5 minutes.

Before serving add chopped parsley, cream if liked and season well.

For a lower calorie version omit cream and just serve with a swirl of single cream

Tony Watson is Chairman of the Tarbat Discovery Centre. He has never been busier since retiring early from his chemist shop in Tain so that he could enjoy more time in the garden! Everyone appreciates the fact that as Chairman of the Tarbat Discovery Centre he is doing a wonderful job.

strathdon soup

serves 6

Contributor: David Lauritsen

90g (3¼ oz) butter

1 diced onion

60g (2½ oz) diced leek

60g (2½ oz) diced parsnip

60g (2½ oz) flour

1 litre (approx 2 pints) chicken stock

500ml (approx 1 pint) double cream

200g (¾ oz) grated strathdon cheese

40g (1½ oz) grated gruyere cheese

150ml (just over ¼ pint) medium sherry

seasoning

Melt the butter & gently fry the vegetables to soften.

Add the flour. Continue to fry gently for 2 minutes,

Add the chicken stock slowly, stirring all the time to prevent lumps occurring.

Bring to the boil then simmer.

Add the cream.

Beat in the cheeses.

Remove from the heat.

Liquidise and sieve.

Return to a clean pan, add the sherry.

Season and serve.

David Lauritsen, the owner of Food Frenzi, is himself a very accomplished chef and often produces mouth-watering dishes for Taste of Tain events. His delicatessen offers a wide selection of local and international food and wines as well as the chance to relax in comfortable surroundings while enjoying superb coffees and excellent food. For further relaxation you can pop next door to David's wife Susan for some really pampering beauty treatments!

bacon, prawn & cheese paté

serves 4

Contributor: Carole Herd

75g (3oz) cooked shelled prawns (chopped)

3 rashers bacon (if you are in a hurry ready cooked is fine)

tub of philadelphia cream cheese

clove of garlic peeled and very finely chopped

freshly ground black pepper

a good squeeze of lemon juice

small bunch of parsley – chopped

If using raw bacon fry until crisp, drain on kitchen paper and put aside until needed.

Put cream cheese, lemon juice and black pepper in food processor and whiz until smooth. Add garlic and parsley and transfer into a bowl. This can be done in the morning and kept in fridge until ready to serve.

Five minutes before serving break bacon into small pieces and add to cream cheese mix along with the chopped prawns. Mix well and serve with melba toast or brown bread.

Garnish with wedges of lemon and sprigs of parsley.

Sometimes I leave out the prawns and bacon and use it as a party dip or to make a more substantial starter I serve it alongside smoked salmon.

I, like most people from this part of the world, am a huge fan of cookery writer Claire Macdonald, and the above is adapted from one of her recipes. I'm asked without fail for the recipe every time I entertain.

Carole Herd, looking for adventure, took part in a sponsored cycle across Cuba in aid of Deaf Children in 2002 and raised over £4000 for the charity. As part of her fundraising she organised a dinner/auction at a nearby hotel. She enjoyed the experience of the dinner/auction and impressed by the wealth of riches and talent Tain has to offer went on to organising the first ever Taste of Tain event.

smoked mackerel paté

serves 4

Contributor: Tanya Brooke

2 smoked mackerel fillets

1 pot cream cheese

juice of ½ lemon

1 teaspoon horseradish sauce

garlic clove - crushed

salt and pepper

parsley – chopped

Couldn't be easier! Put all the ingredients into blender and blend until smooth...

Originally from New Zealand and married to Charlie Brooke, Tanya cares very much for the community as a whole and holds many charitable events in her home.

chicken liver paté

serves 6   *Contributor:* Cathy Shankland

2 packets chicken livers

1 onion

3 cloves garlic

2 tablespoons of crème fraiche

olive oil or large knob of butter for frying

juice of half a lemon

1 tablespoon of brandy

1 bay leaf

salt & pepper to taste

Chop up and fry onion and garlic gently until soft and translucent.

Add chicken livers and bay leaf and fry until cooked through but not overdone - about 10 minutes.

Remove bay leaf, put into liquidiser with the crème fraiche and lemon juice and whiz until smooth.

Stir in brandy and season to taste.

Cathy learned to knit at her grandmother's knee. Now addicted to knitting for its therapeutic as well as creative qualities she makes knitted accessories, using traditional elements with a contemporary twist.

game paté with green peppercorns

serves 6   *Contributor:* Prue Douglas-Menzies

170g (6oz) cooked game meat

110g (4oz) butter

100ml (4 fl. oz) whipping cream

1 small clove garlic

1 small onion

2 teaspoons green peppercorns

2 tablespoons brandy

1 bay leaf

salt and freshly ground black pepper

lemons for garnish

Melt the butter over low heat.

Finely chop the onion and add to the butter with the bay leaf - fry until the onion is golden brown.

Add the brandy and remove the bay leaf.

Put the mixture into a food processor, add the game meat and blend until very smooth.

Place the mixture in a bowl and stir in the peppercorns.

Whip the cream until it stands in soft peaks and fold it into the mixture.

Season well and place in pots or a single dish. Chill.

Garnish with quarters of lemon and serve on hot toast.

serves 2-4   *Contributor:* Jamie Stone (MSP)

blewits

gather 275g (½ lb) of wood blewits 'lepista nuda' which grow, not in woods, but - surprisingly - in short grass near the sea (at least in the highlands) during September and October (as to the exact identification of the wood blewit, best to get someone who knows to show you. That was what I did all those years ago).

1 tablespoon unsalted butter

1 cup double cream

dry sherry or dry white wine

salt & black pepper

thick sliced brown wholemeal bread

butter

chopped fresh parsley

Chop the blewits into pieces approximately 12mm to 25mm (1/2 to 1") square and fry them in a tablespoon of unsalted butter on a medium heat.

Cook until they are lightly browned.

Add one cup full of double cream and a dash of dry sherry or dry white wine, plus salt and ground black pepper to taste. (actually, go easy on the pepper - while blewits have a unique, slightly scented flavour, it is only too easy to obliterate it with too much seasoning.)

When the mixture is a pale shade of golden brown, and slightly thicker than the cream originally was in its tub (on pouring it into the pan, it will initially have become much more runny) take the pan off the ring and park it on the side of the stove. You're almost there.

Make the toast - preferably brown wholemeal, and thick - butter it, and spoon on the blewits and cream.

Chop and sprinkle the smallest bit of parsley, and serve!

Bon appetit!

Jamie's tip: If you ain't got blewits - Flora and I didn't find any this year - ordinary mushrooms will do.

This is one of Flora's and my favourites. It costs virtually nothing, apart from the cream, and everyone says 'yum yum'.
Jamie Stone is the local member of the Scottish Parliament.

serves 2   *Contributor:* Susannah Stone

chicory
french mustard
a little chopped ham
grated cheese

Boil chicory for about 10 mins.
Cut in half and place in baking dish.
Mix together French mustard, cream, grated cheese and a little chopped ham if you like.
Spread the mixture over the chicory and bake in the oven for 20 minutes.

black pudding with blue cheese dressing

serves 2

Contributor: **Pat Gibson**

2 slices black pudding

2 rashers streaky bacon

bunch of watercress

1 juicy pear

cube of blue cheese

2 tablespoons crème fraiche/mayonnaise

1 slice bread for croutons

Cube bread, drizzle with olive oil and bake on tray in oven until crisp.

Grill bacon until crisp. (This can be done in advance).

Wash and pick over watercress and put to drain on paper towel.

Grill black pudding for 2-3 minutes each side.

Dressing

Home made mayonnaise is best but if you prefer something less fattening mix 2 tablespoons crème fraiche with a little vinegar to the consistency of single cream.

Crumble the cheese and add to the mixture, stirring gently.

Peel and core pear, cut in half lengthwise, and then cut each half into 3 lengthwise.

To serve: Arrange croutons on plates. Pile watercress on top. Place black pudding edge down and leaning onto cress on one side and 3 pear strips on other side. Finish off with blobs of dressing over the top. Enjoy!

Pat Gibson is a Community Councillor in Tain.

mussels cooked in oatmeal

Contributor: **Roddy Robertson**

fresh mussels

medium size oatmeal

salt and pepper

butter

slithers of garlic

Wash mussels in cold water and put into pan of boiling water. Boil until shells open.

Throw away any that haven't opened.

Flick flesh out of shell into polythene bag with oatmeal, salt and pepper and gently shake until mussels are well coated.

Melt butter in frying pan along with slithers of garlic.

Add mussels and continue cooking until the oatmeal starts to brown.

Delicious!

Roddy got the idea for this recipe after visiting an old lady on the west coast of Scotland. She had nothing in the cupboards to give him to eat, and being a very Highland lady wouldn't let him leave without offering something, so she went out to the beach at the back of her house, gathered up some cockles, and cooked them in the same manner as the recipe above.

Roddy, a local businessman and farmer, was born in Tain and takes a keen interest in the well being of the Tain community. He has served on the Town Council as Senior Bailie and is Chairman of the Community Council as well as being an Honorary Sheriff and Justice of the Peace. He is also Provost of Tain.

smoked salmon or trout tinbals

serves 4

Contributor: Jean Paterson

225g (8oz) smoked salmon

2 eggs

small tub fromage frais

chives

lemon rind from small lemon

salt, pepper, some sunflower oil

Whiz all the above ingredients together in a blender.

Line small ramekin dishes or small tins with oiled cling film and then cover with tin foil.

Steam for approximately 15-20 minutes.

The Moray Firth is one of the best firths for salmon; it has a very firm flesh and delicious flavour. The above is a recipe I use quite often.
The history of salmon fishing and the Paterson family go back many years. Jean's delicious recipe for Salmon Tinbals is easy to do and well worth a try!

smoked salmon or trout savoury tartlets

serves 6

Contributor: Prue Douglas-Menzies

smoked trout filling

1 smoked trout

60g (2oz) full fat soft cream cheese

15g (½ oz) soft butter

1 dessertspoon mayonnaise

1 teaspoon lemon juice

salt and freshly ground pepper

small quantity chopped parsley

Skin and bone trout.

Place in food processor with the butter, cheese, mayonnaise and lemon juice.

Blend until smooth.

Season to taste.

Fill tartlet cases and sprinkle with chopped parsley.

Note: small pastry cases can be very time consuming to make and are now available in packets (not frozen) in various sizes from supermarkets.

Prue is well known for her charity work, award winning honey and for being one of the best cooks in the county. Her recipes have always been kept a closely guarded secret and Taste of Tain feel very privileged that she has agreed to release a few for this book.

favourite recipes...

MAIN COURSES

ILLUSTRATION BY RICHARD EASSON

The Delny House Hotel

roulade of beef with smoked salmon & hramsa in a red wine sauce

serves 2-4

Contributor: Graham Rooney, Head Chef, Delny House Hotel

red wine sauce

454g (1 lb) mixed carrot, celery, onion and fennel

trimmings and beef bones

pig's trotter

1 clove garlic

1 teaspoon coriander seed and black peppercorns

1 bay leaf

2 teaspoons tomato puree

1 litre (over 2 pints) chicken stock

500ml (a little over a pint) red wine

50g (2oz) cold diced butter

roulade of beef

200g (7oz) fillet of beef

30g (1oz) smoked salmon

30g (1oz) hramsa cheese

salt and pepper to season

hramsa cheese

to make 454g (1lb) of hramsa

4 litres (approx 1 gallon) of whole milk

5 tablespoons natural yoghurt

2 tablespoons chopped wild garlic

salt and pepper to season

Note: serve roulade of beef carved, and served with red wine sauce and fresh garden vegetables.

Red wine sauce

Finely chop the carrot, celery onion and fennel. Mix together.

Brown the beef trimmings, bones and pig's trotter.

Add the finely chopped vegetables, garlic, spices and tomato puree.

Cook on a medium heat for ten minutes until browned.

Add stock and red wine and bring to the boil.

Skim off the scum and simmer for two hours.

When simmering is complete, strain the stock and reduce to the consistency of a sauce

Check seasoning.

Whisk in the cold butter.

Roulade of Beef

Place the fillet of beef between two sheets of cling film and beat with a heavy meat bar until about 5mm (1/4 inch) thick taking care not to tear the cling film.

Season the beef and layer with the smoked salmon and hramsa cheese.

Roll into a sausage shape.

Seal the meat in a hot pan.

Place in a pre-heated oven 180 degrees C (350 degrees F) or Gas Mark 4 for approximately 5 minutes.

Take the roulade out of the oven and rest in a warm place.

Hramsa cheese (courtesy of Susannah Stone)

Place the milk and yoghurt into a pan and leave in a cool place until a cream has formed on the top.

Remove the cream and place the pan beside a heat source (e.g. a lit hob) Keep the mixture warm until it has thickened naturally. Overnight is ideal.

Once thickened, cook the mixture over a medium heat until the mixture resembles scrambled egg.

Place the mixture into a muslin strainer and hang, allowing it to drip dry, for approximately 3 to 4 hours.

Finally, mash the cheese and add fresh chopped garlic.

Season to taste.

Graham Rooney is head chef of the **Delny House Hotel** and has recently been awarded the 2005 bronze medal winner at the prestigious Salon Culinaire d'Ecosse awards ceremony held in Glasgow. This was the biggest Salon event ever held in the UK.

Hramsa cheese is an old Highland crowdie. In the days of the old Highlander it was known as Gruth with fresh wild garlic. It is believed that Crowdie, which is low in fat and of course an extremely healthy option, has always been made in Tain and the surrounding area of the Highlands. Susannah Stone, Celtic Fine Foods and founder of Highland Fine Cheeses

balblair angus whisky pepper steak

serves 2

Contributor: **Lesley Whitlaw**

whisky pepper sauce

1 tablespoon butter

2 tablespoons chopped white onion

2 cups beef stock or canned beef broth

¼ teaspoon cracked black pepper

1 clove garlic, pressed

2 tablespoons of single scotch malt whisky

1 green onion, chopped

1 teaspoon cornstarch

1 tablespoon water

pepper steaks

1 x 454g (16oz) sirloin steak, cut into two portions

2 teaspoons cracked black pepper

2 tablespoons butter

salt

Firstly, fire up the barbecue for the steaks.

Whisky pepper sauce - Prepared on the kitchen hob.

In a saucepan or deep skillet, make the whisky pepper sauce by sauteing the white onions in the butter over high heat. In about 3 minutes the onions will begin to turn brown.

Add 1 cup of the beef stock to the onions. Add the cracked black pepper and garlic at this point as well.

Continue to simmer over medium/high heat until the sauce has reduced by about half.

Add the whisky, green onion, and remaining 1 cup of beef stock to the sauce and let it simmer over low heat while you prepare the steaks.

When the steaks are just about done, combine the cornstarch with the tablespoon of water in a small bowl. Stir just until the cornstarch dissolves.

Remove the whisky sauce from the heat and add the cornstarch to it.

Put the sauce back on the heat and continue to cook on low until the sauce is thickened to the consistency you desire.

Serve the steak doused with Balblair Elements pepper sauce.

Pepper steaks

Spread 1/2 teaspoon of cracked pepper over the entire surface of each side of the sirloin steaks and press into the steaks so that it sticks.

Melt 2 tablespoons of butter in a large skillet over medium/high heat.

Drop the steaks into the melted butter and sear each side of the steaks for 1 & 1/2 - 2 minutes or until brown.

When the barbecue is good and hot, grill the steaks for 3 - 5 minutes either side or until they are done to your liking.

Salt the steaks lightly as they grill.

Lesley Whitelaw, Brand Manager, Balblair Distillery.

Founded in 1790 Balblair is one of the oldest working distilleries in the industry. It is situated in one of the most beautiful parts of the country, where the Ross-shire burns flow down the Struie Hill to the farm lands of Edderton, the "parish of peats" and down onwards to the shores of the Dornoch Firth.

Balblair Distillery is very supportive of the local community and events, where they often hold very popular Whisky Tasting Classes!

steaks with whisky cream sauce

Contributor: Alasdair Rhind

2 fillet steaks

2 slices bread

81 g (3oz) butter

1 teaspoon french mustard

1 teaspoon flour

1 shallot

3 tablespoons water

½ cup cream

2 teaspoons chopped parsley

1 beef stock cube

1 tablespoon whisky

1 teaspoon lemon juice

Cut bread into rounds the same size as steaks.

Heat 27g (1oz) butter in pan, add mustard and mix well.

Brush bread on both sides with this mixture, place on baking tray and bake in moderate oven for 20 minutes, or until golden brown.

Heat remaining butter in pan, add steaks and cook until done as desired.

Remove from pan and keep warm.

Drain pan leaving one tablespoon of fat.

Add flour and finely chopped shallot.

Stir over heat for a few seconds.

Stir in water, bring to the boil then add cream, parsley, crumbled stock cube, whisky and lemon juice.

Reduce heat and simmer for 2 minutes.

Remove bread from oven, place steaks on top and pour over sauce.

steak & stilton

Contributor: Mandy Rhind

4 sirloin steaks

4 oz stilton cheese

1 tablespoon butter

2 tablespoons mango chutney

salt and black pepper

Preheat grill and trim steaks.

Mash cheese and butter together and stir in mango chutney.

Season steaks on both sides and grill as required.

Spread cheese mixture over steaks and return to grill for 1 minute.

Serve immediately.

Alasdair Rhind has been involved in the Tain community for the past twenty years. Being in business in Tain, he firmly believes in putting back into the community what he takes out and has spent much of the past twenty years helping to promote and improve the community for one and all. Councillor and Chairman of many committees in the town, he encourages many who he works with, and ultimately achieves the aspirations of the community. Married to Mandy they have three children who all enjoy the beauty of Tain and its surrounding area.

highland cattle beef cooked swedish style (tjaelknoe)

Contributor: Alan Torrance

highland cattle beef
cold water
salt
sugar
pepper
bay leaves
juniper berries

Take a piece of frozen meat.

Put it in the oven at 75°C to 90°C (165°F to 198°F) - - Gas Mark 1/4.

Slow cook for 10 to 12 hours.

Put a thermometer in the beef - at 72°C (165°F) it is ready.

Put the beef in cold water with 1 part salt to 10 parts water, tenth part sugar, some pepper, some bay

leaves and some juniper berries.

Keep in water for 8 to 10 hours.

Serve cold in thin slices, with cheesy potatoes, vegetables and red wine sauce.

Alan Torrance, Tain Fold Highland Cattle

This recipe came from the late Andy Buchanan, Meggernie Fold, a well known Highland Cattle judge reported having eaten it on a trip to Sweden. It has been cooked several times in Scotland in the Torrance household, using those frozen lumps from the bottom of the freezer, where the labels have dropped off. Whether brisket or salmon cut the recipe always produces superb results and is highly recommended. We can only think it is the quality of the Highland Cattle Beef to start with that makes it a surefire winner!

Highland Councillor Alan Torrance and his wife Susan first started breeding Pedigree Highland Cattle in 1991. Since then they have bred many champions and won lots of prizes. Most of the stock is for Pedigree Breeding but when they do have any beef for sale you have to be quick as being very low in cholesterol it is in great demand.

beef olives filled with haggis & creamy whisky sauce

serves 4

Contributor: Head Chef, St Duthus Hotel

8 thin slices of sirloin steak or minute steak
2 haggis
onion
whisky
gravy beef
double cream

Beef olives

Take your thin slices of beef open up your haggis break it up to fit each sirloin & roll into sausage shapes.

Seal each olive in a frying pan with olive oil.

Then place them in an ovenproof dish, drizzle with olive oil & cook for 25 - 30 min.

Sauce

Fry onions with the whisky, add gravy, salt & pepper, when hot add double cream then pour over your olives & serve.

Lovely accompanied with carrots, turnip & roast potatoes

Head Chef, **St Duthus Hotel**

Located centrally to the town the St. Duthus, a family run business has everything a person could need - comfortable bedrooms, excellent menu in bar/restaurant and friendly staff..

serves 4

Contributor: Connie Beaton

beef

500g (1¼ lb) stewing steak cut into cubes

27g (1oz) plain flour

1 teaspoon dried mixed herbs

salt and pepper

1 chopped onion

3 tablespoons oil

110g (4oz) baby carrots

2 parsnips, quartered and sliced

I pint beef stock

110g (4oz) frozen peas

cobbler (topping)

250g (8oz) self-raising flour

pinch salt

54g (2oz) butter/margarine

1 egg beaten plus extra for glazing

3 tablespoons milk

Beef

Toss the meat in a mixture of flour, herbs and seasoning.

Cook in the oil until browned.

Transfer to a casserole.

Cook the onion in the oil until soft and add to the casserole with the carrots, parsnips and beef stock.

Season to taste.

Cover and cook in a moderate oven 160°C (325°F) - Gas Mark 3 - for 2 hours until the meat is cooked.

Stir in the peas.

Cobbler (topping)

Sift the flour and salt into a bowl.

Rub in the fat until the mixture resembles fine breadcrumbs.

Stir in the beaten egg and enough milk to make a soft dough.

Roll out on a lightly floured work surface to about 25mm (1") thick.

Cut into rounds using a scone cutter.

Place the cobblers on top of the meat in the casserole.

Increase the oven heat to 220°C (425°F) - Gas Mark 7 and bake for 15 minutes.

Apart from being a keen tennis player and a talented member of the Flower Club, Connie's tasty recipe for Beef Cobbler proves that she is also a very good cook.

supper or lunch with left over haggis

serves 4

Contributor: Hazell Gill

left over haggis

left over turnip

left over potatoes

1 large onion or 2 small ones

Fry onion until brown and caramelized.

Put a layer of haggis on the bottom of an ovenproof dish.

Follow with a layer of onion and a layer of turnip and finish with a layer of potatoes.

Put in the oven and cook until piping hot.

chicken with whisky sauce

serves 4   *Contributor:* Father Andrew & Imelda McMichael

25g (1oz) butter

60g (2oz) shredded leeks

60g (2oz) diced carrot

60g (2oz) diced celery

4 shallots, sliced

600ml (1 pint) chicken stock

6 chicken breasts

50ml (2 fl oz) whisky

200ml (7 fl oz) low fat creme fraiche

2 tbsp freshly grated horseradish *or*

1 tbsp ready made horseradish sauce

1 tsp honey, warmed

1 tbsp chopped fresh parsley

salt and pepper

parsley to garnish

Melt the butter in a large saucepan and add the leeks, carrot, celery and shallots.

Cook for 3 minutes, add half the chicken stock and cook for approx 8 mins.

Add the remaining chicken stock and bring to the boil.

Add the chicken breasts and cook until tender.

Remove the chicken with a perforated spoon and cut into thin slices. Place on a large, hot serving dish and keep warm.

In another saucepan, heat the whisky until reduced by half. Strain the chicken stock through a fine sieve, add to the pan and heat until the liquid is reduced by half.

Add the creme fraiche, the horseradish and the honey.

Heat gently and add the chopped fresh parsley and salt and pepper to taste.

Place original vegetable mix onto plates and use as a cushion for the chicken which should be placed on top.

Pour a little of the whisky sauce around the chicken and pour the remaining sauce into a sauceboat to serve.

After cooking with stock and vegetables, chicken breasts are served with a velvety sauce made from whisky and low fat creme fraiche.

To serve: the vegetables which were cooked in the stock, new potatoes, or rice a selection of fresh vegetables.

This is a low fat recipe and not only is it good for you - it tastes wonderful!

A carved mouse is the trade mark of Robert Thomson of Kilburn Yorkshire who furnished the interior of St. Andrews Episcopal Church. There are seven elusive mice hidden in various parts of the building. Father Andrew, the Priest in Charge, found all but one which he discovered just before this publication.

castlecraig chicken salad

serves 12-20

Contributor: Liz Whiteford

250g (8oz) finely chopped onion

2 tablespoons oil

2 level tablespoons mild curry powder

275ml (½ pint) chicken stock

4 level teaspoon tomato puree

juice of 1 lemon

8 level tablespoons apricot jam

6 tablespoons double cream

275ml (½ pint) mayonnaise

275ml (½ pint) salad cream

1.5kg (3lbs) cooked cold diced chicken

Fry onion in oil until soft.

Add curry powder and cook for 1 minute.

Stir in stock, tomato puree, lemon juice, and apricot jam - bring to boil and simmer for 10 minutes.

Allow to cool.

Add cream, mayonnaise, and salad cream.

Finally add chicken.

Serve with a rice salad or as a filling for baked potato.

Note: *Freezes well.*

Liz takes a great interest in the community and has helped set up and run many projects. She is responsible for the authorisation of Duke of Edinburgh Awards in Ross and Cromarty as well as being a Research and Development Officer for a local company.

tasty crispy chicken

serves 4

Contributor: Murray Macleod

1 x 1.5 kg (3lb) chicken

54g (2oz) butter

2 packets crisps (plain and salt & vinegar)

110g (4oz) grated strong cheddar cheese

¼ teaspoon garlic powder

½ teaspoon dried tarragon

salt and pepper to taste

Quarter chicken - cut more or less portions depending on the size.

Melt butter and brush chicken joints.

Crush crisps in the bag and then mix in plastic bag with remaining ingredients.

Place the mixture over the chicken in a casserole dish.

Place in pre-heated oven 180°C (350°F) - Gas mark 4 - for approximately 50 minutes.

Test with probe to ensure chicken is cooked through.

Murray Macleod is the founder member of the 1st Tain Highland Gathering in 1993. One year on, following a sponsorship with Glenmorangie Distillery, the Gathering became known as Glenmorangie Tain Highland Gathering. This annual event is now rated one of the premier Highland Games and Gatherings in the north of Scotland.

chicken broccoli bake

serves 4   *Contributor:* Maggie McAuley

1 large broccoli

2 cooked chicken breasts

2 medium potatoes

1 x 300g (10oz) tin condensed chicken soup

3 tablespoon mayonnaise

½ cup of milk

2-3 teaspoon curry powder

grated cheese for topping

Preheat oven to 180°C (350°F) - Gas mark 4.

Shred the cooked chicken breast and put aside.

Peel and cut potatoes into 1cm (1/2 ") slices; dissect broccoli into florets and cook both of these for about 1 minute until just tender (you could steam the broccoli on top).

Make the sauce in a large bowl - thoroughly mix the soup, mayonnaise, milk and curry powder.

Spread half of the sauce at the bottom of a casserole dish then layer shredded chicken, broccoli and potatoes in that order and pour remaining sauce all over the top.

Cook in the oven for 15-20 minutes.

Remove and sprinkle grated cheese over the top and grill until golden.

Serve with salad and French bread.

This recipe is a tasty favourite of *Maggie McAuley* and one she has shared with her readers in an early issue of the Tain and Dornoch Picture Post's 'Recipe Corner'.

Maggie McAuley took over as editor of the Tain & Dornoch Picture Post, a local monthly magazine, in January 2004 having been sub-editor for a year and a half previously. The TDPP was created in February 2000 by Tain photographer, Mr. Murray Macleod and it proved to be extremely popular. It is a magazine primarily devoted to the Dornoch Firth area although it has over the years gained retail outlets in the Cromarty Firth area. It covers local news and events and has a variety of regular contributors such as short story writers, reports from local organisations, writers of local history and so forth which gives readers a variety of content. It has a large focus on pictures taken from local events and the "Old File" historical pictures are extremely popular. Communication is one of the main functions of the magazine and readers are encouraged to view it as a platform to air their opinions or request exposure of particular ventures. It has become hugely popular, particularly in Tain, since its inception and has become a 'collectors item' for many local readers.

chicken carol-land

see below

Contributor: Lorraine Christy

allow 1 chicken breast fillet per person

allow half a banana per person

allow 2 smoked streaky bacon rashers per person

Preheat oven to 180°C (350°F) - Gas mark 4.

Flatten out the breast fillet, wrap around the banana, then stretch the bacon and wrap around the chicken.

Place in oven on a baking tray.

Cook for 15 - 20 minutes or until the juices run clear.

Serve with a salad and crusty French stick or rolls.

The carol-land can also be barbecued. Wrap the parcels in cooking foil. Cook in the embers until the juices run clear. Serve as above.

Note: can be eaten hot or cold

Lorraine Christy works at the Co-op, Tain.
The Co-op are very supportive of local events and throughout the year raise money through weekly raffles etc. for local charities and good causes. Members of staff also help by taking part in sponsored walks, bike rides etc. Tain Co-op promote their Fair Trade Products whenever possible so that countries less well off than ourselves get a fair price for their work and produce.

coachhouse chicken

serves 3

Contributor: Iain Mackenzie

54g (2oz) butter

I desertspoon honey

1 dessertspoon wine vinegar

2 teaspoon dried mustard

1 desertspoon dried marjoram

1 crushed garlic clove

6 skinned chicken thighs/drumsticks

Melt ingredients together and pour over 6 skinned chicken thighs/drumsticks.

Place in pre-heated oven 180°C (350F) - Gas mark 4 - for approximately 40 minutes.

Iain Mackenzie started making quality garden furniture with a difference in the year 2000 and since then has gone from strength to strength. His popular garden seat which quickly turns into a table and bench is ideal for barbecues and outdoor eating. Iain usually finds himself rushing home to the workshop from any Taste of Tain events - just to keep up with the orders!

chicken summer salad

12 oz cooked chicken

1lb new potatoes, cooked and sliced

1 large lemon (or 2 if small)

3 tbs vinegar

6 tbs oil

¼ pt double cream

1 bay leaf

1 sprig of tarragon, marjoram or rosemary

parsley to garnish

Squeeze the lemon and slice the remainder.

Mix the juice with vinegar, oil, the herbs, some salt and pepper and mix with the chicken.

Put the sliced lemon bits over the top and leave to marinate for a minimum of 2 hours.

Meanwhile cook the spuds, cool and slice.

When ready, discard the marinade and mix the chicken with the potato and cream, set it off with a bit of parsley and serve.

A very simple and easy recipe using good, basic ingredients and a couple of herbs from the garden (or the supermarket).
Recipe from *Tain Library.*

wild boar terrine with apricots & prunes

serves 4   *Contributor:* David Graham, Head Chef, The Glenmorangie Highland Home at Cadboll

parma ham - approximately 12 slices

1 kg (2.2lbs) wild boar meat trimmed

75mls egg whites

750mls double cream

1 bunch chopped parsley

100g cooked apricots (soaked in armagnac/brandy and then chopped)

100g cooked prunes (soaked in armagnac/brandy and then chopped)

1wild boar fillet cut lengthways

salt and pepper to taste

Line terrine mould with cling film.

Then line with the Parma ham leaving an overhang.

Ensure all of the fat is trimmed off the wild boar meat and mince or blend in a food blender.

Make sure that all ingredients are as cold as possible when using them to prevent the mixture from splitting. Slowly add the egg whites and then pour in the cream in a steady drizzle.

Add the mixture to a chilled bowl and fold in the chopped apricots, prunes and herbs.

Set aside and chill.

Heat a frying pan with a small amount of oil and quickly seal the boar fillet and season; leave to cool.

Fill the terrine mould halfway with the mixture and then place the boar fillet in the middle of the terrine.

Continue to pour on the mixture until the terrine is filled to the top.

Then fold the Parma ham strips over the top.

Wrap in cling film and tin foil and place in a Bain-Marie (water bath).

Put into the oven for approximately 45 minutes at 190°C (375°F) Gas Mark 5 until a core temperature of 82° is reached.

seared glenmorangie whisky and citrus marinated loin of roe deer with beetroot dauphinoise, wilted spinach and grand veneur sauce

serves 6   *Contributor:* David Graham, Head Chef Glenmorangie Highland Home at Cadboll

beetroot dauphinoise

8 maris piper potatoes
4 fresh beetroot cooked
500ml (1 pt) double cream
1 clove garlic
1 onion chopped
seasoning to taste

grand veneur sauce

4 finely chopped shallots
butter
4 tablespoons white wine vinegar
crushed black peppercorns to taste
250ml (½ pint) game/veal sauce
double cream

marinade for venison

2 oranges squeezed
2 lemons squeezed
6 sprigs thyme
4 garlic cloves
½ onion chopped
1 carrot chopped
1 stick celery chopped
1 large glass glenmorangie single malt whisky
6 x 200g (7oz) pieces venison loins
wash and pick 2 packets spinach

Beetroot Daupinoise

Sweat the garlic and chopped onions in butter and cream and reduce by a third.

Slice a thin layer of potatoes in a greaseproof tray followed by a thin layer of passed cream.

Next a layer of sliced beetroot and continue process until full.

Bake at 190°C (375°F) Gas Mark 5 for at least 40 minutes until set..

Grand Veneur Sauce

Sweat 4 finely chopped shallots in butter.

Add 4 tablespoons of white wine vinegar and reduce by half.

Add crushed black peppercorns to taste and half a pint of game/veal sauce.

Finish with a touch of double cream, and pass through a sieve.

Marinade for Venison

(Only marinade for 4-6 hours otherwise it will become too strong.)

Pat dry the roe deer or venison.

Heat a saute pan with a little oil until almost smoking, seal the deer quickly and season.

Place in a hot oven, 190°C (375°F) Gas Mark 5 for 10 minutes approximately.

Take meat out and rest for 5 minutes in warm place.

Gather all accompaniments and place meat in the oven for a further 10 minutes until medium rare,

Cooking time depends on the thickness of the meat and your preferred degree of cooking.

The meat should always be rested.

Meanwhile sweat the spinach in butter, season and drain.

Garnish with seasonal vegetables.

As Head Chef of the highly acclaimed and award winning **Glenmorangie House**, David leads his small team to deliver supreme quality to the operation. He maximizes the wealth of quality local Scottish produce with his modern Scottish style and often likes to add some Italian influences throughout his dishes, especially fresh pasta.

David very much enjoys his current role as a large part of this includes interacting with many of Glenmorangie's guests who come from a wealth of different backgrounds and cultures.

venison steaks with a port & orange sauce

serves 4   *Contributor:* John Munro Butcher

8 small saddle steaks / 4 small haunch steaks

25g (1oz) butter

1 tablespoon olive oil

50g (2oz) dried sour cherries

juice of an orange

1 shallot (finely chopped)

150ml (¼ pt) port

150ml (¼ pt) venison/chicken stock

2 tablespoons redcurrant jelly

1/2 teaspoon dijon mustard

salt & pepper

Soak dried cherries in orange juice for 1 hour.

Dry the steaks.

Heat butter and oil in frying pan.

Fry the steaks for about 2-3 minutes each side (longer if you wish), then place on a warmed plate while you make the sauce.

Add the shallot to the pan & cook gently.

Drain off any excess fat and add the port, stirring well.

Let this reduce to almost nothing and then add the stock, orange juice and cherries.

Boil until reduced by half.

Add the redcurrant jelly & stir until dissolved.

Taste and adjust seasoning.

Pour over the steaks before serving.

venison stew

serves 4   *Contributor:* Mrs Hazell Gill

2 -3 onions

venison steak (I usually use a haunch) sliced and cut in pieces

seasoned flour for coating

salt and pepper

worcester sauce

tomato puree

1 teaspoon gravy powder

Fry onions until brown.

Remove and keep warm.

Dip venison pieces in flour seasoned with plenty salt and pepper and fry until brown.

Put in an ovenproof casserole along with the onions.

Make gravy with remaining fat and meat juices by adding left over flour and 1 teaspoon of gravy powder, a

dash of Worcester sauce and 1 tablespoon tomato puree.

Pour into casserole and place in a pre-heated oven for 1 to 1 & 1/2 hours at 180°C (350°F) - Gas Mark 4.

Adjust seasoning to taste.

Being a farmer's wife Hazel is always busy baking or cooking and has the knack of making it look effortless. Her recipe for venison stew was one of her fathers and is loved by everyone who tastes it.

duck breasts with redcurrant jelly & port sauce

One prepared duck breast per serving

Contributor: Tony Watson

cooking oil

half chopped onion

small quantity chopped mushrooms

flour

redcurrant jelly

red wine

balsamic vinegar

water or beef stock

salt and pepper

Duck

Wipe breasts clean.

Score fat in both directions and place on very hot griddle, skin side down

Leave to sizzle until the fat runs and the skin side is nicely browned.

Reserve some fat for making sauce.

Take off heat and turn breasts to skin side up.

Cover with foil and put in oven at 190°C (375°F) - Gas Mark 5 - for about 10 minutes.

Leave to sit for 10 minutes before serving with sauce.

Sauce

Put a small amount of duck fat or cooking oil (if preferred) in small pan.

Gently fry onion and mushrooms until soft.

Stir in flour, cook for one to two minutes.

Add redcurrant jelly, red wine, and a flash of balsamic vinegar to taste.

Add some water or beef stock, if needed and cook for a couple of minutes

Season with salt and pepper.

Serve with good mashed potatoes and lots of green vegetables, and of course, a good red wine!

This is a very quick and easy dinner dish.

ducks with grapes & herbs

serves 6 *Contributor:* **Prue Douglas-Menzies**

3 ducks

350g (12oz) seedless grapes

2 tablespoons redcurrant jelly

1 teaspoon thyme for each duck

1 teaspoon sage for each duck

2 teaspoons cornflour

1 wine glass of red wine

1 shallot

salt and pepper

Heat the oven to 185°C (370°F) - Gas Mark 4

Rub the ducks with salt.

Prick the skin.

Sprinkle with herbs and add a little inside each bird.

Put the ducks on a rack in a baking tin, or on the wire shelf of the oven with a roasting tin beneath to catch the dripping.

Put about 20mm (¾") water in the tin with the giblets and shallot.

Roast in the oven until the birds are cooked (about 1½ hours)

Cut the ducks into portions and place in a hot dish and keep warm.

Pour off the fat from the juices in the tin and remove the giblets (I pour it all into a bowl and squirt the juices back into the tin with a baster).

Stir in the wine, redcurrant jelly and grapes.

Slack the cornflour in water and stir into the sauce until it thickens.

Adjust the seasoning and pour over the duck.

juicy **pheasants** with apples & calvados

serves 4-6

Contributor: Prue Douglas-Menzies

2 large pheasants

60g (2oz) unsalted butter

6 shallots

1 small wine glass of calvados

4 large cox's apples

300mls (½ pt) good chicken stock

bouquet garni

200mls (7 fl.oz) cream

seasoning

Melt the butter and brown the pheasants on all sides.

Finely chop the shallots, add to the pan and cook until golden.

Pour the calvados over the pheasants and flame, cook a little to reduce.

Peel and slice the apples and add lo the pheasants with the stock, bouquet garni, and seasoning. Cover, bring lo the boil and simmer for 50 minutes until pheasants are cooked.

Take out the pheasants, carve them into portions and place on a hot serving dish.

Remove the bouquet garni then liquidize the contents of the pan.

Return to the pan, add the cream, adjust the seasoning, heat and pour over the pheasants.

One of the most delicious ways of cooking pheasant and most of the cooking can be done in advance. Calvados is such a good cooking liqueur it is worth the expense.

pheasant casserole

serves 4

Contributor: Liz Mackenzie

1 pheasant

1 tablespoon flour

salt & pepper

25g (1 oz) butter

½ tablespoon oil

1 large onion

170g (6 oz) chopped mushrooms

1 green or red pepper

70ml (⅛ pt) white wine

70ml (⅛ pt) chicken stock

70ml (⅛ pt) double cream

1 tsp lemon juice

Joint the bird and cut breasts into serving portions.

Toss joints in seasoned flour and fry lightly in butter and oil until golden brown.

Place pheasant portions in ovenproof casserole and keep warm.

In remaining fat lightly fry onions, mushrooms and pepper.

Add wine to vegetable mixture and bring to the boil.

Add this to the casserole.

Season to taste.

Mix stock and cream and pour over pheasant and vegetables.

Add lemon juice.

Cover and cook in oven at 180°C (350°F or Gas Mark 4) for 40 minutes until tender.

Nobody went hungry on the Ladies Discussion Group's Day Out when Liz was in charge. She would arrive on the bus armed with a big box full of very tempting home made goodies to nibble and at the end of the day, go home with it completely empty.

loin of lamb with chantrelle rosti

serves 4

Contributor: Chris Driver, Head Chef, Skibo Castle

4 x 150g (5½ oz) lamb loin
(ask your butcher to trim this for you)

4 medium carrots (peeled)

4 x green leaved savoy cabbage
(trimmed into 7cm (2 ½") squares)

4 baking potatoes

400g (15oz) fresh winter chantrelle
(or a mushroom of your choice) wash
and pat dry

250g (8oz) washed spinach leaves

3 eggs beaten

1 litre (1¾pts) of good lamb stock

large glass of red wine

4 shallots chopped

sprig of thyme

squeeze of lemon juice

butter

salt/pepper

fresh chervil

olive oil

Sauce
Take the good lamb stock, red wine, shallots and thyme and simmer until reduced to sauce coating consistency.

Correct seasoning, add a little lemon juice, strain and keep warm.

Rosti
Steam or simmer the potatoes in their jackets for 12-15 minutes, peel whilst still warm, grate and season this mixture.

In a 15cm (6") non-stick pan saute the mushrooms, place on the side. Repeat this process with the spinach.

Heat two 15cm (6") non-stick pans add a knob of butter, then evenly distribute the potato mixture into the pans, press down with the back of a spoon and cook until golden.

On one of these potato cakes layer the mushrooms, then spinach - seasoning each layer.

Carefully turn the other potato cake on top of the spinach - golden side should face up.

Gently press down and cover with the egg mixture, cook in the oven for 20 minutes at 180°C (350°F) - Gas Mark 4.

Lamb
Season the lamb well and seal in a hot pan with a little oil and butter.

Colour evenly and baste at regular intervals - it should take 6 minutes for nice pink lamb.

Remove from the pan and set to one side to rest for about 3 minutes.

Vegetables
Turn the carrots into barrel shapes and cook in boiling salty water until tender. Cook the cabbage in salted boiling water for 3 minutes, put to the side.

To serve: *Portion the rosti, carve the lamb and garnish with the vegetables, sauce and a sprig of chervil.*

Chris Driver, Head Chef, **Skibo Castle**

Chris has competed and won many awards in various competitions around the country. Being no stranger to 5- star establishments and having worked with celebrity chef Steven Saunders of 'Ready Steady Cook' fame he is ideally suited for his position as Head Chef of one of the world's most exclusive private clubs. Hidden away in a romantic Highland landscape of contemplative beauty, Skibo provides luxurious hospitality, magnificent links golf and traditional country sports for a discerning membership.

taste of tain kebabs with ceilidh couscous & aldie watercress salad

Contributor: Robert Hudson

kebabs

½ kg (1 lb) neck fillet of "ross-shire" lamb cut into inch cubes (approx)

3 tablespoons olive oil

3 tablespoons white wine vinegar

1 tablespoon fresh rosemary (or 1 teaspoon dried)

6 rashers of "petley" (easter eoss produce) back bacon cut into approx 1 inch x 2 inch strips

1 small tin pineapple chunks in juice, drained

2 medium sized cooked beetroot cut into pieces the same size as the pineapple chunks

couscous

140g (5oz) couscous

250mls (½ pt) of boiling water

half red pepper finely chopped

half green pepper finely chopped

5 dried apricots finely chopped

2 tablespoons toasted cashew nuts

12 black olives rinsed and halved

1 tablespoon olive oil

salt & freshly ground black pepper

watercress salad

a good bunch of watercress, washed and trimmed

1 ripe sweet pear, cored, quartered and sliced

extra virgin olive oil

salt & freshly ground black pepper

1 teaspoon freshly squeezed lemon juice

parmesan shavings

2 tablespoons chopped walnuts

Kebabs

Make a marinade by mixing the oil, vinegar and rosemary.

Pour over the lamb and leave for at least one hour (Preferably 4 hours in the refrigerator).

Meanwhile, prepare the couscous as instructed in the recipe below.

Assemble the remaining ingredients into kebabs by threading onto skewers as follows: - lamb, beetroot, bacon (fold the bacon pieces in half to make inch squares) and pineapple.

Repeat the sequence until the skewer is full.

Brush with marinade and grill slowly, turning several times.

Whilst grilling the kebabs the watercress salad can be prepared.

Couscous

Put the couscous in a large bowl and pour over the boiling water.

Leave until the water is absorbed, then fork through.

When cool, add the remaining ingredients and mix thoroughly.

Leave to cool or refrigerate in warm weather.

Watercress salad

Place the watercress and pear in a bowl and drizzle with oil, seasoning and lemon juice.

Toss together.

Sprinkle with nuts and parmesan.

Enjoy...

Robert Hudson, Tain Pottery

The Tain Pottery moved into a derelict steading in 1996 on a run down farmyard and is now one of the largest Scottish ceramic manufacturers, with a reputation earned through attention to detail and quality craftsmanship. Their original designs, all hand thrown and painted, continue to evolve with the passing of time … subtle changes effected in the pursuit of excellence. Techniques have been developed by a team of skilled potters with decades of experience to call from. Robert Hudson is a great supporter of the community.

ragout of lamb with red wine

serves 6

Contributor: **Fiona Scott**

56g (2oz) butter

900g (2lb) diced lamb (or boneless leg of lamb, trimmed and cut into 2.5cm (1") cubes)

225g (8oz) unsmoked bacon, as lean as possible, cut into 2.5cm (1) cubes

18 tiny onions, peeled

1 rounded tablespoon flour

285 ml (½ pint) water

420ml (¾ pint) red wine

a bouquet garni

340g (12oz) mushrooms, sliced

salt and freshly ground black pepper

John Scott, Fiona's husband has won many prestigious awards for his prize lambs.

Melt the butter in a heavy casserole, add the lamb and the bacon a few pieces at a time and cook until they are well browned all over.

Remove from the pan to a separate dish and keep warm.

Lower the heat slightly and add the onions. Cook gently, shaking the pan occasionally, until the onions are golden.

Sprinkle in the flour, stir well and cook for a further 2-3 minutes.

Gradually add the water and the wine, stirring all the time until the sauce boils

Replace the meat in the casserole and add the bouquet garni, mushrooms, salt and pepper.

Cover tightly and cook in a moderate oven 180°C (350°F) - Gas Mark 4. for 1 & 1/2 hours.

Remove the bouquet garni before serving.

Serve with mashed tatties (potatoes).

lamb & lentil chilli

serves 4

Contributor: **Lorna Macnab**

1 large onion

2 garlic cloves

220g (8oz) tin of tomatoes

1 small aubergine, diced

½ kg (1lb) diced lamb

150g (5oz) red lentils

1 teaspoon turmeric

2 teaspoons chilli powder

2 teaspoons cumin

1 teaspoon coriander

1 teaspoon brown sugar

1 teaspoon lemon juice

small bunch of coriander chopped

250ml (½ pint) natural yoghurt

Put onion and crushed garlic into 100 ml (approx 1/4 pint) of water in a pan and boil for 5 mins until softened and the water absorbed.

Add remaining ingredients (apart from coriander and yoghurt) and 450ml ((approx 1/2 pint) of water.

Bring to boil, cover and simmer for an hour.

Season and add half coriander and half yoghurt.

Serve with basmati rice and remaining coriander and yoghurt

Lorna is a little bit of a star! There have been many glimpses of her in the television series Monarch of the Glen! She is a very imaginative and tasty cook and given the chance could easily write a cookery book of her own.

easter ross **lamb** with rosemary & onion sauce

serves 6

Contributor: **Mary Mackenzie**

1.95kg (4lb) leg of lamb

slices of garlic

fresh rosemary

herb sea salt

rosemary & onion sauce

tablespoon bruised and finely chopped
rosemary leaves

large chopped onion

26g (1oz) flour

170ml (⅓ pt) milk

170ml (⅓ pt) vegetable stock

2 tablespoons creme fraiche

salt & black pepper

Lamb

Prepare the lamb by cutting small slits in the joint.

Push in a sliver of garlic with a small sprig of rosemary in each slit.

Place lamb in roasting tin, sprinkle with herb sea salt and cover with foil.

Roast in pre-heated oven at about 180°C (350°F) - Gas Mark 4.

Half an hour before finishing remove the foil and continue cooking.

Rosemary & onion sauce

Melt butter & onions over a slow heat and after 5 minutes add the chopped rosemary.

Cook gently for a further 15 minutes.

Stir in the flour until smooth and gradually add the milk stirring continuously - followed by the stock, little by little.

Season with salt & pepper and cook on a very low heat for 5 minutes.

Add the creme fraiche before serving in a warmed jug.

Mary's husband who farms sheep believes it is very important for the lambs to enjoy the freedom of the outdoor life before their inevitable trip to market!

stuffed pork tenderloin

Contributor: John Munro, Butcher

1 x 450g (1lb) pork tenderloin

10 - 20g (½ oz) butter

3-4 rashers streaky bacon

stuffing

25g (1oz) butter

1 onion (chopped finely)

¼ teaspoon thyme

¼ teaspoon sage

75g (3oz) mushrooms (chopped finely)

2 teaspoons lemon juice

1 egg (beaten with 2 tablespoons cream)

Preheat oven to 180°C (350°F) - Gas Mark 4

With a sharp knife, split the tenderloin in half lengthways and flatten the two halves.

Season with salt & pepper.

Stuffing

Melt the butter & fry the onion & herbs for about 10 minutes.

Add the mushrooms & increase the heat. Cook for 4 - 5 minutes until the juices have almost evaporated.

Empty contents of pan into a bowl & add the remaining ingredients.

Fork together and season to taste.

Spoon the stuffing onto one half of the tenderloin & place the other half on top.

Smear the tenderloin with butter & season with freshly ground black pepper.

Cover the top with the rashers of bacon and tie with string.

Bake near the top of the oven for about one hour until ready.

At John M Munro Ltd our philosophy is simple: 'take the finest prime livestock from local farms, and produce the finest matured meats to satisfy our customers' highest standards.'

loin of **pork** in white wine sauce

serves xx   *Contributor:* **Susannah Stone**

1 pork loin

oatmeal

dried apricots

pine nuts

white sauce

cheese

white wine

chopped parsley

Cut loin into 12mm (1/2") thick slices

Roll in oatmeal and fry slowly until oatmeal turns brown.

Put in dish with dried apricots and pine nuts.

Make a white sauce, add cheese and white wine and pour over pork.

Sprinkle with parsley to serve.

Susannah Stone of Highland Fine Celctic Foods,Tain, has always taken a big interest in the welfare of Tain. She is a Community Councillor and serves on many committees as well as being the Chairman of the Tain Heritage Trust, presently raising funds to restore the old Tain Picture House. This is a beautiful building in the centre of town opened many years ago by Andrew Carnegie of Skibo Castle.

Susannah is also the founder of the famous Highland Fine Cheese, which, many years ago, saw local people gathered at Tain station to watch the first batch of cheese being piped onto the train on its journey to London and then rushing home to see themselves on the television news! Her son Ruaraidh now manages the business and has introduced his own award winning cheese – Strathdon Blue. Susannah has set up another business and can always be seen at Taste of Tain events giving delighted customers tastes of her special haggis with its very secret ingredients!

lemon **pork** chops

serves 6   *Contributor:* **Joannie Whiteford**

6 lean trimmed pork chops

brown flour

rounds of apple

lemon slices

½ cup water

½ cup tomato ketchup

2 tablespoons brown sugar

little fat for browning

Dredge chops with brown flour and brown.

Drain off fat.

Put into a dish with a round of apple and a large lemon slice on each chop.

Mix water, tomato ketchup, and brown sugar and pour over chops.

Bake uncovered in a moderate oven for approx three-quarters of an hour.

Joannie is a whiz on the computer and spends time helping and advising others how they too can become computer literate. She proves to be a tough opponent when playing against her at the Tain Tennis Club.

mussels in two sauces

serves 4   *Contributor:* Frank Mahon

3 tablespoons olive oil

1.25kg (3 lbs) fresh mussels in shell, scrubbed

tomato sauce

2 cloves garlic, crushed

125ml (¼ pint) white wine

3 tablespoons tomato paste

white sauce

25g (1oz) butter

30g (1½oz) flour

250ml (½ pint) milk

topping

3 tablespoons grated mozzarella

2 tablespoons grated parmesan

Mussels

Heat half the oil in a large pan.

Add the mussels and cook over high heat, shaking the pan, for 5 minutes until opened.

Discard any that do not open.

Strain the liquid and reserve.

Let the mussels cool, then remove from their shells and set aside.

Preheat the oven to moderately hot 190°C (375°F) - Gas Mark 5 and proceed with the sauces.

Tomato sauce

Heat remaining oil in a pan. Add garlic and fry until golden.

Add the wine and reserved liquid and simmer gently for 5 minutes.

Mix the tomato paste with 3 tablespoons of water, then whisk into the simmering liquid.

Simmer for a further 10 minutes and season to taste with salt and pepper.

White sauce

Melt the butter in a pan.

Add the flour and cook for 1 minute.

Very gradually, stir in the milk over a low heat until the sauce thickens.

Season to taste.

To complete

Combine the tomato sauce and mussels and pour into 4 ramekins.

Spoon over the white sauce, sprinkle with combined cheese and bake for 20 minutes.

mussels with sun dried tomatoes

serves 4   *Contributor:* Frank Mahon

2kg (4¼ lbs) fresh mussels in shell

50ml (2 fl ounces) white wine

450g (1Ib) fresh tagliatelle

4 tablespoons olive oil

50g (2oz) sun-dried tomatoes, chopped

2 tablespoons chopped parsley

salt

Pour the wine into a large saucepan with a tight fitting lid, place over a medium heat and when steam starts to rise add the mussels to the pan and cover with the lid.

Steam for approximately 5 minutes, stirring occasionally.

Whilst mussels are steaming, set a large saucepan of salted water to boil and begin cooking tagliatelle for about 5 minutes or until just tender.

Remove the saucepan of mussels from the heat and pick out three of the best looking ones to leave in their shells and use as a garnish. Remove the rest from their shells and keep warm.

Heat the olive oil and quickly fry the chopped sun-dried tomatoes until they are heated through.

Drain the cooked tagliatelle thoroughly and add to the saucepan, toss to combine with the tomatoes and to coat the pasta in oil.

Stir in the cooked mussels.

Arrange the finished pasta on a large serving dish and garnish with the chopped parsley and reserved shell-on mussels.

Serve immediately.

Mussels are a healthy and versatile eating option and can be used in many ways as either a meal or an accompaniment to a meal. When eating mussels, Frank Mahon prefers them simply steamed or boiled and then eaten piping hot.

Frank heads up a small, family-run business, involved in harvesting, marketing and transporting shellfish, mainly mussels. In the late fifties, Frank helped his mum and dad run a small shellfish outlet in Glasgow and then became involved in the Tain mussel fishery in 1970. With the help of sons, Alan and John, the business has grown, now employing six people. At one time the mussel harvest was bagged in 25kg sacks and sold. Nowadays, based at Meikle Ferry Point, the harvest is cleaned and graded using special mussel cleaning machines imported from France and Holland. They are packed to customers requirements and sold throughout the UK and into Europe.

stuffed mussels

serves 4

Contributor: Frank Mahon

stuffed mussels

1kg (3lbs) large mussels

stuffing

2 cloves garlic, finely chopped

1½ tablespoons parsley, finely chopped

60g (2½ oz) fresh grated hard cheese

2 tablespoons fine breadcrumbs

2 eggs

1 tablespoon olive oil

salt and pepper

Prepare the mussels for cooking, place them in a large pan with 3 tablespoons water, cover and place over a high heat to make them open.

Keep the mussels in their half shells, discarding the empty halves.

Transfer to a large shallow fireproof dish containing 100ml (1/4 pint) water cook gently for 4 minutes.

Mix all the ingredients for stuffing together very thoroughly and leave to stand for 5 minutes

Heap a small amount of this stuffing on top of each mussel.

Place under a preheated grill and cook for about 5 minutes or until brown and crisp on top.

lemon & garlic prawns

serves 2

Contributor: Carole Herd

12 king prawns in their shells

110 ml (4 fl oz) olive oil

juice of 1 large lemon and grated zest of ½ lemon

2 cloves of garlic (crushed)

1 teaspoon salt

coarsely ground black pepper

2 oz (50g) butter

Line a grill pan with foil and arrange the prawns in their shells on top.

Mix together the oil, lemon juice, zest, crushed garlic, salt and pepper.

Whisk everything together and pour the mixture over the prawns.

Leave to marinate for at least an hour.

When ready to cook pre-heat the grill to a medium heat and then dot the butter over the prawns.

Place them about 3 inches from the heat and grill turning them frequently.

Cook for about 5 or 6 minutes or until the skin darkens and begins to look slightly brown.

Remove prawns to serving dishes with the hot juices poured over and serve with lots of crusty bread.

fish casserole

Contributor: **Pat Chilvers Steele**

2 tablespoons olive oil

2 onions, thinly sliced

175g/6oz diced bacon

1 red pepper, seeded and thinly sliced

1 yellow pepper, seeded and thinly sliced

125ml /4 fl oz red wine

450g / 1 lb tinned tomatoes

450g / 1 lb new potatoes scrubbed and halved

2 cloves garlic thinly sliced

1-teaspoon thyme

2 bay leaves

salt and ground black pepper

450g /1lb fillet of firm fleshed white fish

225g 8oz squid cut into 12 mm/1/2 inch rings

3 tablespoons fresh parsley finely chopped

Heat the oil in a large flameproof casserole.

Add the onions and garlic and fry over a low heat for 5 minutes.

Stir in the bacon and peppers and cook for 5 more minutes.

Add the wine, tomatoes, potatoes, thyme and bay leaves and season with salt and pepper.

Bring to the boil and then simmer for 15 minutes.

Stir in the fish and squid and simmer for 10-15 minutes or until the fish is cooked.

Just before serving, taste and adjust the seasoning if necessary.

Sprinkle with fresh parsley over the top of the stew.

uncle angus's fish pie

serves 4

Contributor: **Paul Moclair**

12 oz of cod

6 large potatoes

4 oz mushrooms

2 oz grated mature cheddar cheese

½ pint milk

knob of butter

garlic

pepper

Cut the cod up into bite sized pieces.

Slice the mushrooms

Place both in a pan, cover with milk, sprinkle on pepper and poach lightly for five minutes.

Remove fish and place in bottom of casserole dish.

Use the milk to make a thick white sauce then pour over cod and mushrooms.

Boil the potatoes then mash with liberal amounts of milk and butter.

Spoon the mash over the other ingredients, just as you would with Sheperd's pie.

Sprinkle on grated cheddar and bake in oven at medium heat for thirty minutes.

partan pie ~ seasoned crab soufflé in the shell *('Partan' from the Gaelic meaning Crab)*

serves 1

Contributor: Gordon Robertson, Oystercatcher Restaurant.

cooked brown crab

large egg

tablespoonful of thick béchamel [sauce made by heating some milk to a roux (cooked mixture of flour and butter) and mixing well] - to ensure it is smooth either pass through a sieve or beat with an electric whisk

seasonings

pinch of salt

pepper

thai curry powder

and a dash of anchovy essence

garnish

shredded lettuce

sweet smoked paprika

pimento-stuffed olive cut in half and leaf of coriander/flat leafed parsley

extras

lemon & oatcakes/warm buttered toast

Carefully remove the top shell by prising off with a blunt knife [oyster knives are good for this] above the tail flap.

Clean this shell. Break off the flap and discard both this and the gills [easily distinguished as they are the feathery, greyish-coloured "dead man's fingers"].

Break off the claws and legs. Remove all the white and brown meat from the body and the legs and place into a bowl.

Carefully break the claws without completely destroying them [with the back of a heavy knife or rolling pin].

Separate the egg putting the yolk into the crab bowl and the egg white into a fresh bowl. Whisk the egg white until stiff.

Add Béchamel and seasonings to the crab and egg yolk bowl and beat well together, fold in the egg white and spoon this mixture into the cleaned top shell

Bake in a fan-assisted, pre-heated oven at 180 degrees C for 18 minutes or until risen and gently browned but not too dry.

Place on shredded lettuce to help balance, add claws beside it, dust lightly with sweet smoked paprika, add olives halves and coriander on the soufflé to represent its eyes and nose/mouth.

Serve with a lemon wedge & oatcakes/buttered toast fingers [soldiers].

Gordon Robertson, **Oystercatcher Restaurant**.

The Oystercatcher is a renowned, small, Scottish restaurant, located in the picturesque village of Portmahomack, mainly specialising in local seafood. We have a vast array of malts and a very distinguished wine list. This dish uses the local ingredients of the Portmahomack crabs, eggs from Jan's Happy Hennery and oatcakes from local baker Harry Gow.

grilled red mullet on a pea tomato risotto

serves 4

Contributor: David Graham: Head Chef, Glenmorangie Highland Home

4 fillets of red mullet (get fishmonger to pin bone and fillet the mullet)

125g (4½ oz) double cream

100g (4oz) frozen petit pois

salt & pepper

half an onion, chopped

butter

200g (7oz) arborio rice

3 tablespoons dry white wine

500ml (1pint) chicken stock

100g (4oz) cooked fresh peas

20g (1oz) grated parmesan cheese

olive oil

16 sun-dried tomatoes halves, diced

2 sprigs tarragon

balsamic vinegar

Boil double cream and add frozen petit pois.

Season to taste.

Blend and set aside.

Sweat onions in a little butter without letting it colour.

When tender, add rice and cook for a few minutes, stirring continuously.

When the rice is shiny, pour in the wine and cook until absorbed.

Add hot chicken stock a ladle at a time.

Reduce heat to simmer until liquid is absorbed (grains should have a slight bite).

Add fresh peas, parmesan, a tablespoon of butter, pea puree and salt & pepper to taste.

Warm tomatoes with a little olive oil, balsamic vinegar and tarragon leaves

Season the red mullet, brush with olive oil and grill until cooked and the skin has bubbled.

Serve the risotto on warm plates, with the tomatoes arranged round the outside.

Place mullet on top of risotto and serve immediately.

You can put pesto on as well, or caviar is you wish.

David Graham, Head Chef, **Glenmorangie Highland Home**

Tain greatly appreciates having Glenmorangie Distillery on its outskirts. Annette Mackenzie is in charge of the friendly, well stocked shop and visitors centre and is often seen at local events welcoming visitors with little tastes of the great whisky!

scampi provençale

Contributor: Ross Bannerman

450g (12-16oz) peeled scampi

1 onion

1 clove garlic

2 tablespoons oil

450g (16oz) tinned tomatoes

3 tablespoons dry white wine

salt and black pepper

1 level teaspoon caster sugar

1 rounded teaspoon cornflour

1 rounded teaspoon chopped parsley

Rinse the scampi under cold running water and pat them dry on absorbent paper.

Peel and finely chop the onion and garlic.

Heat oil in large, heavy-based pan, add the onion and fry over low heat for about 5 minutes or until soft, but not browned.

Add garlic and scampi and fry for a further 3 minutes before blending in the tomatoes and wine.

Season to taste with salt, freshly ground pepper and sugar.

Bring to the boil and simmer for about 6 minutes.

Blend the cornflour with 1 tablespoon of water and stir into the scampi.

Cook for a few minutes, stirring until the sauce has thickened.

Remove from the heat and add the parsley.

Simple recipe

Defrost the Scampi by rinsing under cold running water and pat them dry on absorbent paper.

Heat a pan on a hot stove and add butter or olive oil.

Add scampi when pan is hot on low heat.

Sauté for 2/3 minutes, tossing them in the pan while cooking.

If preferred add crushed garlic prior to cooking the scampi.

Dry white wine can also be used to deglaze the pan to change the flavour of the sauce.

Do not add salt as it will impair the natural sweet taste.

Ross Bannerman, General Manager: Bannermans Seafoods

A desire to improve the quality of seafood arriving on the tables of Scotland led to the creation of one of Scotland's few remaining independent seafood companies -Bannerman Seafoods of Tain. Formed in the 1900's by Iain and Bob Bannerman this family business specializes in quality seafood from the Highlands of Scotland. There is a 20,000 sq. ft. processing complex, which, automated with full freezing and storage facilities, ensures products produced on the site are to the latest EEC quality, hygiene and safety standards. Bannerman Seafoods export to France, Spain, Greece and the USA.

complimented by a
Black Isle Brewery
& wild garlic beurre blanc.

paupiette of line caught balnagown river **sea trout** filled with a hand~dived moray firth scallop mouse~line

serves 1   *Contributor:* Graham Rooney : Head Chef, Delny House

500g (18oz) scallops

1 egg white

250ml (½ pint) double cream

sea salt

ground white pepper

4 sea trout fillets (scaled & boned)

500ml (1 pint) fish stock

250ml (½ pint) *black isle brewery red kite* beer

1 tablespoon white wine vinegar

2 shallots (finely chopped)

150g (5oz) unsalted butter
(cut into 1cm (½") cubes)

bunch fresh wild garlic (finely chopped)

Preheat the oven to 200°C (400°F) - Gas Mark 6

Reserving four of the scallops as a garnish blend the remaining scallops with the egg white in a blender or food processor.

Gradually add the double cream, until a firm mousse has formed.

Add the seasoning.

Roll the sea trout fillets into cylinder shapes, stand end-on and spoon the mousse mixture inside them.

Place one of the reserved scallops on top of each cylinder and secure with cocktail sticks.

Place the fish in an ovenproof dish with half of the fish stock and cook in the oven for about 12-15 minutes.

Black Isle Brewery & wild garlic beurre blanc

Put the remaining fish stock, Black Isle Brewery Red Kite, white wine vinegar and chopped shallots in a pan and reduce the liquid to approximately 100ml (1/4 pint).

Sieve the reduced liquid and return it to a hot pan, gradually add the cubes of butter to the reduced fish stock.

Remove from heat and whisk until creamy sauce has formed.

Finally, add the finely chopped wild garlic and serve with sea trout.

Graham Rooney, Head Chef, Delny House

'I have travelled the length and breadth of Scotland, getting involved with the raw ingredients of my trade and have learnt the value of using the best produce, properly sourced and freshly cooked. In the summer of 2004 a table of four American lunch guests commented that the trout which they had eaten was the best they had ever tasted. I explained that there is a river just a couple of miles along the sandy beach, which they could see from their window seats and this was where I had caught their lunch at half past six that very morning. It turned out that they had just come from a tour of the Black Isle Brewery, which was also in the dish. They further wondered where the wild garlic came from. This, I revealed, was something to which I had been sworn to secrecy by Mrs. Stone, for whom I picked wild garlic as a young lad.'

salmon patties

serves 6-8   *Contributor:* Janet McKeachan

300g (10oz) potatoes peeled and cut into cube

200g (7oz) salmon, skin and bones removed

2 spring onions finely chopped

3 tablespoons chopped parsley

1 tablespoon lemon juice

100g (4oz) dry breadcrumbs

oil for frying

2 teaspoons sweet chilli sauce

plain flour for dusting

2 eggs lightly beaten

Cook potato in boiling water until soft.

Drain and place in large bowl.

Mash until smooth.

Add salmon, spring onions, chopped parsley, sweet chilli sauce and lemon juice.

Mix to combine.

Divide mixture into 8 equal portions.

Shape into round patties with wet hands.

Coat each patty lightly with flour

Dip each one in beaten egg

Coat with breadcrumbs.

Cover with cling film and chill for 1 hour.

Heat oil in frying pan.

Fry patties for about 4 minutes each side until golden brown.

Janet McKeachan, Gizzan Briggs, Tain Royal Academy

Kathryn Wilkie, Roddy McLean, Mairead Simpson and *Jimmy McLean* started **Gizzen Briggs** approximately 12 years ago in Tain Royal Academy. At first it was just an excuse for a group of pupils and staff to get together to play some traditional music. Shortly after that however, we gave our first public performances in Tain and have never looked back.

Gizzen Briggs has travelled three times to Montana, USA; playing the length and breadth of the state. Gizzen Briggs enjoy a following there and have made live radio broadcasts, played in the Governor's state mansion, performed during the 4th of July celebrations and performed at ceilidhs too numerous to mention, throughout the state. The group is always well received and the pupils have been excellent ambassadors for the town, the Highlands and indeed the whole country.

We have produced one tape and three CDs over the last ten years, with thousands of copies sold all round the world - one was even tracked down to a music shop in Alaska. The reason for Gizzen Briggs' existence has never changed and although the players may change year on year, our intention is still to give pupils the opportunity to play and perform traditional music and to bring that music to the community. Most recently, Gizzen Briggs were asked to play at the official opening of the new Scottish Parliament building at Holyrood on the 9th of October 2004, an invitation we were delighted to accept, on behalf of ourselves and on behalf of the community of Tain.

Jimmy McLean, Chairperson, Gizzen Briggs

salmon fish cakes with tartare sauce

serves 6

Contributor: **Trish Geddes**

tartare sauce

2 tablespoons capers - chopped

2 small pickled gherkins - chopped

2 tablespoons chopped chives - mayonnaise,
lemon juice and pepper

mix ingredients together and pour into small
serving dish

fish cakes

454gm (11b) salmon fillet

454gm (11b) potatoes

half teaspoon anchovy paste

lemon juice

2 tablespoons fresh coriander

1 egg

flour

breadcrumbs (made in processor)

Peel, boil and mash potatoes, leave to cool.

Cook salmon by placing fillets into small roasting tin,
squeeze lemon juice over the top and season with salt
and pepper.

Add little water and cover with foil.

Bake in oven at 200°C (400°F) - Gs Mark 6 - for 10 minutes
and leave to cool.

In bowl place mashed potatoes and flaked salmon,
anchovy paste, lemon juice and chopped coriander.

Mix well together and form into 12 fish cakes.

Dip each fish cake into flour, then beaten egg and finally
breadcrumbs brown or white - whichever you prefer.

Leave in fridge for 1 hour to set.

Shallow fry for 4-5 minutes on each side until golden brown
and keep warm in oven.

Trish Geddes is a wonderful cook and does so for a living as well as treating her friends to mouth watering home baking and tasty meals. She also plays a very active part in the community and being a beautiful singer is a member of the Garrick Singers, the Choral Society and the Last Gasps whose performances throughout the year are always thoroughly enjoyed and well attended.

salmon morangie

serves 4

Contributor: Brian Campbell, Head Chef Morangie House Hotel

4 salmon steaks weighing 227gm each (8oz)

227gm (8oz) mussel meat

250ml (½ pint) white sauce

227gm (8oz) butter

227gm (8oz) flour

250ml (½ pint) milk

juice of one lemon

2 teaspoons garlic

1 onion

1 bunch parsley

2 teaspoons dried mixed herbs

1 glass white wine

salt and pepper

White sauce

Melt butter.

Add the flour and stir until mix leaves the side of the saucepan.

Gently heat the milk and add to the butter and flour.

Mix, stirring the sauce occasionally.

Bring to the boil and leave to one side off the heat

Handy tip

If white sauce has gone lumpy pass through a strainer

Prepare salmon

Lightly brush an oven tray with butter.

Place salmon fillets onto tray

Brush salmon with butter, lemon and parsley.

Morangie sauce

Place about a tablespoon of oil into a saucepan and heat gently.

Finely chop onion and place into saucepan.

Cook slowly till onion is soft.

Add garlic, mixed herbs, lemon juice and white wine.

Cook for a further 3-4 minutes.

Add white sauce.

Slowly cook and finally add mussel meat.

Taste and check for seasoning.

Add salt and pepper as required.

Cook salmon

Pre-heat oven to 180°C (350°F) - Gas mark 4.

Put salmon in oven for 20 minutes.

To serve: put salmon fillet onto a plate and spoon sauce over the salmon. Make sure you get plenty of mussel meat over the fish. Garnish with a wedge of lemon and a sprig of parsley.

Brian Campbell, Head Chef, **Morangie House Hotel**

Brian arrived at the Morangie House Hotel to take up the position of Head Chef in 1997. He believes that the choice of fresh produce to be found on the hotel's doorstep can not be bettered and has chosen this dish for the Taste of Tain cookery book as he believes the wild salmon from this area to be the best.

dave's memorable salmon steaks

serves 4

Contributor: David Macdonald

4 salmon steaks, or fillets off the bone

1 jar cajun spices.

Coat salmon in Cajun spices - use the whole jar between the four steaks/fillets.

Slap onto a very hot plate or frying pan with butter and completely blacken each side.

Serve with new potatoes.

David Macdonald, Morangie Garden Centre

David catches his own salmon locally and has tried many ways of cooking them but the above is his favourite.

grilled salmon

serves 4

Contributor: Charles Brooke

4 x 170g (6oz) salmon fillets

2 tablespoons extra virgin olive oil

225gm (8oz) soft goat's cheese

salt & pepper

dill

Preheat grill on high.

Brush both sides of fillets with oil and season with salt & pepper

Place fish skin side up on grill pan and cook for 3-4 minutes.

Turn fillets and spread or slice goat's cheese over the fish.

Season again.

Put back under grill until cheese bubbles & is golden in - approx. 4 minutes.

Garnish with fresh dill.

Serve at once.

Twenty five years ago Charlie returned from Yorkshire, where he had been working in the family wool mill, to live at home with his father. Charlie had read about fish farming and was very interested and keen to introduce aquaculture to the farm agenda.

There was a burn with a steady and clean source of fresh water and this supply has been crucial to the development of the fish farm over the years. Charlie was passionate about the concept that the world market was demanding a higher yield of fish and yet the fishing fleets were reducing wild stocks and causing endless controversy with their nets and hauls. Quite simply the health conscious want to eat more fish at the right price.

Charlie has long since ceased to farm trout and now concentrates on salmon alone.

mike's marinated salmon

serves 2   *Contributor:* **Mike Herd**

2 salmon fillets

freshly squeezed lemon juice

olive oil

freshly ground black pepper

Serve hot or cold.

Half an hour before cooking season fillets with black pepper and place in a dish.

Pour a little olive oil on top followed by a squeeze or two of lemon juice and leave to marinate.

Turn once.

Cook in a very hot frying pan or on a barbeque.

So simple, yet delicious!

Mike Herd could have lived anywhere, just as long as he was near an airport but enjoyed the quality of life Tain has to offer.

His travels as a wildlife director/cameraman have taken him all over the world and into some of the most remotest places on earth. He was the first person in the world to film Sunderban Tigers in the Swamps of Bangladesh and spent many an uneasy night in a hide to do so. All worth while as he came home with an award winning film which has been shown on the National Geographic Channel many times! Living away from home and being no cook he had to rely mostly on other members of the team for his meals!. Mike's recipe comes from his Russian guide Igor who did all the cooking while he was filming Grizzly Bears of Kamchatka for the Discovery Channel. It certainly made an impression on him as he took notes on how Igor cooked the salmon and now won't have it any other way!

Kebabs with ceileidh couscous & aldie watercress salad

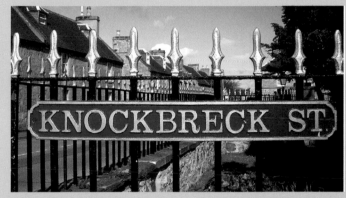

Brambles

(Below) Partan pie & (right) The Oystercatcher Restaurant

Scotsburn Road

Mr Carnegie's dining room at Skibo Castle

Right - Loin of lamb with chantrelle rostis

Immediate right
The Murray monument

Far right
A reverse view from the High Street showing
Tain's Courthouse and the Royal Hotel

Looking south-east along Tain's High Street

Tain High Street

Berets by Cathy Shankland

Jewellery by Lucy Woodley

Stafford Street looking towards Tain conversation area

Bags by Karen Livingstone

Locally made garden furniture by Ian Mackenzie

Knockbreck House

Mansfield Castle Hotel

The famous Tain Tolbooth

One of the fine early stained glass windows in the Collegiate church

Glenmorangie House, Cadboll

Loin of roe deer

Delny House Hotel

Fillet of Balnagown seat trout

mediterranean pasta

serves 4   *Contributor:* Lucy Ballantyne

125g (4½ oz) dry pasta
(we like to use spaghetti)

1 small red onion, finely chopped

8-10 sun dried tomatoes, roughly chopped

10 pitted green olives, halved

10 cherry tomatoes, halved

small tin of tuna, drained and flaked*

approx 12 fresh basil leaves, chopped

2 tablespoons extra virgin olive oil

sea salt and freshly ground pepper

Boil pasta for 20 minutes, until cooked, then drain and set aside.

Mix onion, tomatoes, olives and tuna in a bowl adding oil and seasoning.

Add bowl mix to pasta, followed by the basil leaves and mix together until heated through over a medium heat.

Note! This recipe contains tuna; if you are a strict vegetarian, *please disregard this recipe.*

Serve hot or cold.

Lucy Ballantyne is a professional illustrator, and works at The Tain Pottery as one of their team of pottery decorators and produces the pottery's stock designs as well as one off originals and bespoke commissions. She also undertakes freelance illustration work and very kindly offered to do some of the beautiful illustrations which are scattered throughout this book showing once again how the community pulls together for special events.

A self confessed "foodie", Lucy enjoys travelling to sample the culinary delights of foreign lands as well as good Scottish produce. The above recipe is one she often makes for her husband Derek, and is a quick, easy, and healthy dish, delicious served hot or cold.

stuffed pumpkin with cheese & white wine sauce

serves 2   *Contributor:* Susannah Stone

1 pumpkin
sliced mushrooms
red onion chopped
cheese and white wine sauce
grated parmesan cheese

Halve the pumpkin and remove pips.

Stuff each half with sliced mushrooms and finely chopped red onion

Make a white wine sauce – add cream and pour over mushrooms.

Season and bake until pumpkin is soft.

Sprinkle with grated Parmesan Cheese.

peasemeal pakora

serves 4 *Contributor:* Ian Smith, Caledonian Curry Company

250g (8oz) sieved peasemeal

1 teaspoon cayenne pepper

1½ teaspoons ground fenugreek

1 teaspoon ground coriander

1 teaspoon salt

250ml (½ pint) natural yoghurt

warm water to mix

300g (10oz) cooked and flaked haddock*

1 tablespoon chopped fresh coriander

oil for deep frying

Put all the dry ingredients in a bowl and mix well.

Stir in the yoghurt.

Add warm water until the mixture is smooth and thick.

Gently fold in the flaked fish and the chopped coriander.

Heat oil to150°C(350°F).

Place spoonfuls of the mixture into the oil and cook until golden brown.

Drain on absorbent paper and serve hot with a yoghurt raita.

*Note! This recipe contains haddock; if you are a strict vegetarian, *please disregard this recipe.*

Enjoy!

Chef *Ian Smith* of the **Caledonian Curry Company,** has been creating gourmet quality fusion ready meals in the Northern Highlands since 1997. By using local venison, beef, game, shellfish and lamb he has created a unique range of additive and gluten free ready meals and has won many accolades for his efforts to enhance fine local ingredients with Indian cuisine.

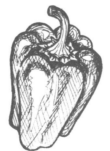

vegetable pasta

Contributor: Margaret Urquart

250 g (9 ozs) fusilli

1 small to medium carrot - cut into matchsticks

1-2 sticks of celery – sliced

half of a green pepper – sliced

half of a red pepper – sliced

125 g (4½ oz) mange tout – sliced

a few mushrooms – sliced or quartered

4 medium to large tomatoes – chopped

1 medium to large onion – chopped

1-2 teaspoons mixed herbs

¼ teaspoon chilli powder or cayenne pepper

freshly grated parmesan cheese

Note: the choice of vegetables is flexible. The list here can be added to or some items substituted to make use of small amounts of raw vegetables left over - green beans, runner beans, small cauliflower florets, fennel etc.

In a large non-stick frying pan or wok, on a high heat, fry the onion for 1-2 minutes stirring constantly.

Stir in the mixed herbs and spice then add the prepared vegetables and stir for 5 minutes

Add the chopped tomatoes and heat through.

Season with salt and freshly ground black pepper.

Meanwhile cook the pasta (3 minutes only, if fresh).

Drain pasta and either stir into vegetable mixture or serve pasta with mixture spooned on top.

Serve with grated parmesan cheese.

Margaret Urquart, Tain-Through-Time

"Ask a busy person if you want anything done" This is certainly true of Margaret who is more than happy to lend a hand gardening town plots, watering street flowers, working in the museum and anything else that needs done. In 2002 she walked the Inca Trail and raised over £4000 for Marie Curie.

Tain Through Time is a four star visitor attraction administered by Tain and District Museum Trust. It consists of 3 buildings contained within a churchyard whose gravestones date back to at least the 17th century and probably further. The buildings comprise of a Medieval Church, the Collegiate Church of St. Duthus, a Museum with a variety of artefacts gathered from Tain and surrounding district over many years in display cases, the Pilgrimage Building which uses dramatic paintings and murals to illustrate 1000 years of history from the time of St. Duthus up to and including the Reformation with special emphasis on Tain's role as a Pilgrimage centre in the Middle Ages.

vegetarian lasagne

serves 6   *Contributor:* Fiona Robertson

sheets of lasagne

1 tablespoon oil

2 onions - chopped

½ red pepper - chopped

½ green pepper - chopped

110g (4oz) mushrooms - sliced

110g (4oz) tomato puree

110g (4oz) mature cheddar cheese - grated

350g (14oz) tin tomatoes

¼ pint water

1 teaspoon mixed herbs

1 teaspoon paprika

salt and pepper

50g (2oz) butter

50g (2oz) flour

500ml (1 pint) milk

Heat oil in a pan and saute the onion until soft.

Add the peppers and mushrooms and cook for a further 2 minutes before adding the tomato puree, tinned tomatoes, herbs, seasonings and water.

Simmer for 15 minutes, stirring occasionally.

Pour a thin layer of the sauce into the base of an ovenproof dish, cover with a layer of lasagne and repeat

the layers of sauce and lasagne, finishing with a layer of lasagne.

Melt the butter in a saucepan, blend in flour and cook for 2 minutes.

Remove from heat and stir in the milk.

Return to the heat and bring to the boil, stirring until the sauce thickens.

Add cheese, salt and pepper and pour over the lasagne.

Grate some extra cheese and sprinkle over the top.

Bake for 35 minutes in the oven 190°C (375°F) - Gas Mark 5.

Note: you can use any other vegetables of your choice. I just use up what I have readily available and sometimes add a tin of kidney or baked beans to give it bulk.

Fiona Robertson, Community Development Project Officer

One of Tain's many strengths is the commitment and enthusiasm of volunteers within the community who are willing to give of their time, skills and experience in order to create and sustain a positive community. The community appreciates Tain's wonderful environment and recognises with responsible care and use it provides a resource for better employment, enjoyment and life-chances for themselves and coming generations. Fiona works with all the voluntary groups to develop various economic, environmental and social projects for the benefit of the whole community.

favourite recipes...

PUDDINGS

ILLUSTRATION BY RICHARD EASSON

plate apple pie

serves 6

Contributor: Mrs Edith Ross

454g (1lb) cooking apples

5 tablespoons flour

2 tablespoons cornflour

2 tablespoons caster sugar

1 teaspoon baking powder

1 egg beaten

125g (4oz) butter or margarine.

Cook apples, sweeten then cool.

Mix dry ingredients, rub in butter and add beaten egg.

Roll out and divide in two.

Put one round on plate, add apples and put other round on top.

Seal well then prick with fork.

Keep pastry in from edge as it expands in the cooking.

Bake at 220°C (425F) - Gas Mark 7 - until golden brown.

If you want to know anything about old Tain, apart from going to the museum, *Edith Ross* is the person to ask. Edith takes a keen interest in the history of Tain and one could easily spend a few days looking through all the photographs and interesting pieces of information she has kept over the years.

When visiting the Collegiate Church Tain you will see a small plaque to the memory of Edith's aunt, Dr. Elizabeth Ness MacBean Rose, who voluntarily gave her life during the European war to help the typhus stricken Serbian soldiers.

spiced pears

serves 6

Contributor: Hazel Gill

6 whole pears with skins removed

175g (6 oz sugar)

4 fluid ounces(100 ml) water

2 inch stick of cinnamon

paired rind of 1 lemon

Cook all the ingredients in a pan for 10 minutes.

Add 1/2 cup red wine.

Simmer for 1/2 hour until pears are soft.

Remove Pears and place in serving dish.

Boil the remaining liquid to reduce and pour over the pears.

Serve cold.

Note: This dish freezes well.

scottish fruit tart with whisky

Contributor: **Craig Eccleson**

pastry
350g (12oz) sweet shortcrust pastry

finely grated zest of 1 lemon

filling
100g (4oz) soft dark brown sugar

100g (4oz) butter

1 tablespoon golden syrup

2 medium eggs, beaten

grated zest of 1 lemon

100g (4oz) currants

50g (2oz) sultanas

50g (2oz) raisins

50g (2oz) walnuts, chopped

2 tablespoons whisky (or juice of 1 lemon)

Once the pastry has been made, with the addition of grated lemon zest, leave to rest for 20minutes before rolling.

Roll the pastry 2-3 mm (about 1/2 inch) thick and line a 20cm (8") flan ring, pressing gently into the edge for a neat finish.

Leaving it untrimmed, refrigerate for a further 20 minutes.

Pre-heat the oven to 200°C (400°F) - Gas Mark 6.

The top edge of the pastry can either be left hanging over during cooking - to trim once baked - or be pressed and trimmed for a 'pinched' finish.

Line the ring with greaseproof paper, fill with baking beans or rice and cook in the pre-heated oven for 15-20 minutes.

Remove from the oven and lift the paper and rice or beans from the case.

For the filling reduce the oven temperature to 190°C (375°F) - gas mark 5.

Gently melt the sugar, butter and golden syrup in a saucepan.

Remove from the heat and whisk in the beaten eggs.

Add the lemon zest fruits walnuts and whisky.

Mix all together well and spoon into the pastry case.

This can now be baked for 20-25minutes.

Remove from the oven and leave to relax.

This tart can be served warm or cold and served with cream custard or Ice-cream.

This is a typical British tart, its Scottish origins betrayed by the addition of whisky. The enclosing of dried fruit in pastry is very similar to the Scottish black bun, a cake made especially for New Year. And this tart would be perfect for Christmas, New Year, or any time of the year. If you're not a big fan of whisky it can be omitted from the recipe and replaced with the juice of a lemon. The whisky can be offered separately, served whipped into double cream or custard.

The Royal Hotel enjoys an enviable situation at the end of Tain High Street. It is the perfect place to enjoy the weekly playing of the Tain Pipe Band or any other activities which are taking place on the High Street while having a drink in one of the comfortable lounges. Head Chef Craig Eccleson and his team have a reputation to be proud of and wherever possible like to use traditional Scottish fayre.

monteagle raspberry pudding

serves 8

Contributor: Helen Jones

Note: best to make the day before required

900g -1 kg (2lb) raspberries

180g - 225g (6-8 oz) sugar - according to taste

½ pt (250ml) whipping cream

½ pt (250ml) natural yoghurt

10Og (4oz) demerera sugar - for topping

Melt sugar over raspberries over gentle heat, taking care not to break rasps up too much.

Cool before placing in glass bowl.

Whip cream and fold in natural yoghurt.

Carefully place cream on top of rasps, making sure that juice does not seep up through cream.

Level top and sprinkle demerera sugar on top, covering all with a thickish layer of sugar.

Cover with cling film and leave in fridge overnight.

"Scotland is famous for it's raspberries and this recipe is delicious with the fresh raspberries from Mounteagle's walled garden but even better with frozen, giving the fresh flavour of summer fruits in the depths of winter. Use a pretty glass bowl to show off the colour. This quantity is for an 20cm/8" bowl but adjust the quantities to suit"

This recipe is from Helen Jones, who, together with her husband Richard and son Owen, farm and also run a holiday cottage business called Mounteagle Estate Holidays. Situated in the grounds of the estate, the cottages are luxury 4 star and together with their own private access to Loch Eye - with it's fishing and wild life - offer the ideal base for families looking for activity, or people just wanting to get away from it all.

gooseberry crumble

serves 4

Contributor: Paul Moclair

2 lbs gooseberries

8 oz caster csugar

2 oz butter

4 oz plain flour

Cook gooseberries with sugar.

Sieve and arrange in a baking dish.

Rub butter into flour and sugar to make a crumble topping and sprinkle over fruit.

Bake in a moderate oven for 45 minutes.

Serve with lashings of cream or custard, depending on the weather...

party pudding

Contributor: Connie Morrison

175g (6oz) plain flour sieved

¾ rounded teaspoon baking powder

¾ rounded teaspoon bicarbonate of soda

¾ rounded teaspoon ground cinnamon

¾ rounded teaspoon salt

slightly less than 300 ml (½ pint) sunflower seed oil

350g (12oz) caster sugar

3 large eggs

225 g (8oz) grated raw carrot

oil for greasing.

filling and icing:

175g (6oz) cream cheese

175 g (6oz) butter

225g (8 oz) icing sugar

½ teaspoon vanilla essence.

Sieve all the dry ingredients together.

In a large bowl beat the oil and sugar together.

Add eggs one at a time. Make sure to beat well in between each one.

Fold in the dry ingredients and stir in the grated carrot.

Spoon the mixture into a lightly greased 25 cm (10 inch) round cake tin lined with silicon paper and bake in a moderate oven 350 degrees F (180 degrees C) or Gas Mark 4 for 45 minutes before lowering the heat to 325 degrees F (170 degrees C) or Gas Mark 3 and bake for a further 20 minutes.

When cooked remove the cake from the oven and allow to cool for about 5 minutes before turning out onto a cooling rack. Peel off the paper and leave to get completely cold.

Filling

Beat the cream cheese and butter together.

Add the icing sugar gradually sieving it as you go.

Beat together well and add the vanilla essence.

Split the cake in half and fill and cover with the butter cream.

There are fond memories of first footing *Connie Morrison* and her late husband Alex Morrison, founder of Morrison Construction, on New Year's morning. Usually it was the last port of call because everyone knew that as well as a warm welcome there would be a huge plate of sandwiches, sausage rolls and lots of goodies to eat. It always ended on a happy note with everyone in the mood for a song!

lucy's wicked **chocolate dessert**

serves 10-12   *Contributor:* Lucy Woodley

110g (4oz) shelled hazelnuts

454g (11b) plain chocolate (chopped)

4 tablespoons brandy

500ml (approx 1 pint) double cream

5 tablespoons golden syrup

cocoa powder

chocolate waffles

Grease a 25cm (10") spring-release cake tin and line the base with oiled greaseproof paper.

In a pan under a hot grill, brown the hazelnuts, shaking occasionally to brown all sides.

Put on paper towel and rub off the skins before grilling again until thoroughly toasted.

Cool before putting them in a food processor.

Chop very finely.

Empty into the base of the cake tin.

Put the chocolate, liqueur and golden syrup in a large bowl and stand over a pan of simmering water until the chocolate has melted.

Remove the bowl from pan and slightly cool.

Whip the cream until it just holds its shape.

Fold a little of the cream into the chocolate mixture first, then fold in the remainder.

Pour on top of the nuts.

Give the tin a tap once or twice to remove air bubbles.

Cover with cling film and chill in the refrigerator for several hours until set. If possible leave overnight.

To serve lift the cake out onto a plate.

Dredge thickly with cocoa powder and chocolate waffles.

Designer jeweller *Lucy Woodley* spent her childhood in a small Highland fishing village. The sea and its creatures are a constant source of inspiration in her work. Lucy's latest range incorporates sandblasted coloured glass, reminiscent of flotsam and jetsam from the tide line, set in silver, forging ever-closer links with the marine environment.

serves 10-12

Contributor: Neil Munro

base

125 g (4½ oz) butter

1 egg

1 teaspoon baking powder

80g (3oz) caster sugar

250g (8oz) plain flour

filling

750g (26 oz) quark (available from most supermarkets: quark is similar to fromage frais but not the same so do try and find some quark!)

2 eggs (separate yolk and egg white)

1 teaspoon vanilla extract

125g (4½ oz) caster sugar

2 heaped tablespoons custard powder

juice from 1 lemon

1 small cup of vegetable oil (150ml (¼ pint))

about 500ml (1 pint) milk

Base

Mix flour, sugar and baking powder, add egg and soft butter and mix/kneed to an even, slightly sticky finish.

Grease 25cm (10inch) round baking tin and press dough into bottom and up the sides, keeping the base slightly thicker.

Cover the whole area of the base and sides with little holes using a fork or toothpick.

Filling

Mix Quark, egg yolk, vanilla, sugar to a smooth cream.

Add lemon juice and oil.

Mix custard powder and milk in a separate bowl making sure that there are no lumps left in the bottom.

Add custard/milk to the filling and stir to an even finish.

Beat the egg whites with a little lemon juice until stiff and then carefully add to the rest of the filling.

Put the filling into the baking tin on top of the base and bake at 200 degrees C (400 degrees F) or Gas mark 6 for about 60 minutes.

Cover the cake with baking paper towards the end to keep the top from getting too dark.

After 60 minutes turn the oven off, open the door slightly and allow the cake to cool down inside the oven.

I was delighted but slightly daunted to be asked to contribute a recipe for this book, but I am sure that the one chosen will find many a happy tummy. My partner Anke has agreed to give up her gran's recipe for a traditional German Cheesecake and while it could hardly be described as a local dish all of the ingredients can be found locally and, it does taste great!

'Through active participation in sport, the management and staff of Tain Sports Shop, keep up to date with new developments in the sporting world......... well, it's a good excuse for a game of tennis!'

balblair elements raspberry cheesecake

serves 6   *Contributor:* Lesley Whitelaw

the base

125g (4 oz) butter

250g (8 oz) digestive biscuits

1 tablespoon single scotch malt whisky

the filling

250g (8 oz) cream cheese

65g (2 oz) caster sugar (granulated)

275ml (½ pt) double cream

1 tablespoon single scotch malt whisky

the topping

250g (8 oz) raspberries

2 tablespoons honey

6 tablespoons single scotch malt whisky

3 level teaspoons arrowroot

1 level teaspoon caster sugar 135ml (¼ pt) whipping cream

The base

Melt the butter in a non-stick pan, add the tablespoon of single scotch malt whisky

Crush the digestive biscuits and add to the pan.

Mix well and press into a greased, loose-bottomed 8-inch cake tin.

Chill for about half an hour in the refrigerator.

The filling

Beat the cream cheese and sugar together.

Whip the double cream and single scotch malt whisky until softly stiff and fold into the cream mixture. Spread over the biscuit base and chill.

The topping

Soak the raspberries in the honey and single scotch malt whisky for about 30 minutes.

Strain the raspberries and reserve the juice.

You will need about 100ml (under 1/4pt) of juice and you may have to top it up with whisky

Take half of the juice and mix the arrowroot to form a paste.

Heat the rest of the juice with the sugar until almost boiling and stir in the arrowroot paste.

Continue stirring over a low heat until the glaze is thick.

Stir the raspberries into the glaze and leave until cool.

Spread the raspberries and glaze over the base.

Whip the cream mixed with a tablespoon of single scotch malt whisky until softly stiff and then decorate the cheesecake.

Finally, sprinkle a tablespoon of malt whisky over the top just before serving.

Lesley Whitelaw, Brand Manager, Balblair Distillery

This is a simple cheesecake which uses two ingredients for which Scotland Is well known -Balblair Elements Single Scotch Malt Whisky and Fresh Raspberries. Two thirds of the Raspberries grown in Britain come from Scotland, Instead of Raspberries, you can use other soft fruit such as Blackcurrants or Loganberries. (The quantities below should provide six portions of cheesecake)

iced banana parfait

serves 6

Contributor: David Graham

6 ripe bananas, peeled and chopped

juice and grated zest of 1 lemon

75ml (3 fl ounces) dark rum

12 egg yolks

225g (8oz) caster sugar

600ml (1 pt) double cream

Puree the bananas, juice, zest and rum in processor
till smooth.

Whisk egg yolks and sugar in pan over simmering water.

Whisk till leaves a trail.

Remove bowl from pan and whisk in banana puree.

Whisk cream till soft peaks and gently fold in to banana mix.

Pour into ramekins and freeze.

frozen strawberry & zabaione terrine

serves 6-8

Contributor: David Graham

400g (14oz) ripe strawberries
(can use raspberries)

200g (7oz) caster sugar

½ wine glass sweet red wine

4 egg yolks

250ml (just under ½ pint) whipping cream

Put the strawberries, half the sugar and the wine in a blender
till smooth.

Pour the puree into a terrine mould.

Whisk the egg yolks with the remaining sugar till thick and pale.

Whip the cream till soft peaks form, and fold into the
egg mixture.

Pour on top of the puree.

Freeze for at least 3hrs.

This recipe was requested and made for a very special birthday party being held at Glenmorangie House. Everyone enjoyed it so much that David was inundated with requests for the recipe.

tain summer pudding

serves 4

Contributor: **Melissa Gray**

8 oz fresh raspberries and/or strawberries/
redcurrants

2oz sugar

some stale bread

whipped cream

Boil fruit with sugar until soft.

Cut bread into slices and remove crusts.

Line a pudding basin with bread, then pour in the boiling fruit and cover basin with fairly thick slice of bread.

Press a plate on top and put a heavy weight over this.

Stand overnight, chill and serve with whipped cream.

Melissa Gray discovered the delights of the Highlands when she relocated here in the summer of 2000, after living and working for ten years abroad in Hong Kong and China. Realising that she was duped by that deceptive summer all those years ago, she fervently hopes as a sun worshipper, that this summer will be as long and hot as everyone predicts it to be...

old man schneider's five families tiramisu

serves 4

Contributor: **Paul Moclair**

sponge lady fingers

4 eggs (1 per person is the rule)

4 tablespoons of white sugar

1 mug of real black coffee

250 gms of marscapone cheese

cocoa powder to garnish

Mix eggs with sugar and beat mercillessly for five minutes.

Add the cheese and administer another sound threshing to blend

Dunk the lady fingers quickly into the coffee

Smear a bowl with the mix.

Put down a layer of soaked lady fingers

Pour over a thick layer of the mix

Add another layer of fingers

Pour over another layer of mix...and so on.

Sprinkle with cocoa and leave overnight.

This recipe is contributed in memoriam *to a dear friend, Mr "Old Man' Schneider from my Shanghai days.*
I wish him well wherever he may roam and may he rest in peace. This was one of his favourite recipes and we think of him fondly whenever we can be bothered to make it.

favourite recipes...

BAKING

ILLUSTRATION BY RICHARD EASSON

cranberry bread

Contributor: Tain Royal Academy Community Complex (TRACC)

225g (8 oz) cranberries

½ level tsp salt

2 large eggs

50g (2 oz) melted butter

175g (6 oz) castor sugar

grated rind &. juice of 1 orange

50g (2 oz) chopped walnuts

350g (12 oz) self raising flour

Chop cranberries coarsely.

Sift flour and salt, add sugar and grated orange rind.

Mix thoroughly, make a well in the centre and add eggs, orange juice and melted butter.

Mix well, fold in chopped walnuts and cranberries.

Bake in greased and lined 23cmx13cmx5cm (9x5x2inch) loaf tin at 180C (350 degrees F) or gas mark 4. for 1 hour.

Remove from tin and cool. After 24 hours serve sliced and buttered.

TRACC is responsible for the community use of the facilities at the Academy. The aim is to encourage and promote a wide variety of leisure, sport and recreation to Tain and the wider community including areas covered by Tain Royal Academy's feeder primaries.

quick bread

Contributor: Melissa Gray

1 lb of plain flour

1½ teaspoons baking powder

1 teaspoon of sugar

1 teaspoon salt

½ pint of milk

Sieve flour and baking powder, add sugar and salt and stir in milk *quickly*.

Make into a flat roll and bake on a greased and floured sheet in a hot oven for 15 minutes.

nut bread

Contributor: Alasdair & Brenda Mearns

350g (12oz) malted brown flour

150g (5oz) strong white flour

1 teaspoon salt

1 teaspoon sugar

1 tablespoon chopped nuts

1 tablespoon sunflower seeds

1 x 7g packet yeast

1 tablespoon olive oil (or vegetable oil)

300ml (over ½ pint) warm water -
one-third boiling water, two thirds cold water

sesame or poppy seeds

brush on

1 egg

½ teaspoon salt

50 g (2 oz milk)

Beat lightly and apply as directed below.

Place all ingredients in a large bowl and add the warm water.

Kneed for at least ten minutes.

Shape and cover with 'brush-on' (beat lightly 1 egg,
1/2 teaspoon salt and 50ml/1/8th pint).

Allow to rise in a warm, draft-free area to double original size.

Prior to cooking re-apply 'brush-on' and sprinkle with sesame seeds or poppy seeds.

Bake in pre-heated oven for 30 minutes at 230°C (450°F) - Gas Mark 8.

Alasdair & Brenda Mearns, Alternatives

Alternatives offers an eclectic mix of products and services, mostly based on the interests and inclinations of the owners, Alasdair & Brenda Mearns.

Alasdair Mearns is a fully qualified practitioner of Traditional Chinese Medicine (acupuncture and Chinese herbal treatment) and the shop offers wonderfully relaxing treatment rooms on the lower level. These rooms are also used by various visiting practitioners, such as a massage therapist and hypnotheripist.

To complement the practice, the shop offers sales of herbal supplements, organic and herbal skin and beauty products as well as healthy gift wares.

The Mearns' also enjoy a strong interest in traditional music and so musical instruments are available. Accordions, whistles, fiddles and bagpipes are all on offer, along with accessories – cases, chanters, reeds, etc.

special queencakes

Contributor: Shona Mackay

1 tub yoghurt (any flavour)

3 tubs self raising flour

1 tub caster sugar

1 tub vegetable oil

2 eggs

Empty yoghurt tub into bowl.

Wash out tub and use as a measure for the flour, caster sugar and oil.

Mix all the ingredients together.

Spoon into paper cases.

Bake at 200°C (400°F) - Gas Mark 5 - for 10-15 minutes.

Shona Mackay, The Wool Shop.

The Wool Shop sells knitting yarns, dress and craft fabric, haberdashery, cross stitch kits, tapestry canvases, bridal accessories and much more for the needlework enthusiast.

ginger raisin cake

Contributor: Barbara Rae

225g (8oz) plain flour

3oz sugar

4 tablespoons black treacle (heaped)

or

2 tablespoons treacle and 2 tablespoons syrup (according to taste)

1 level teaspoon bicarbonate of soda

3 level teaspoons ground ginger

110g (4oz) margarine

225g (8oz) sultanas

1 size 2 egg

2 tablespoons lemon juice

150ml (¼ pint) milk

Warm treacle and sugar together gently to liquify.

Cool.

Rub margarine into flour, bicarbonate of soda and ginger.

Add raisins, treacle and sugar, mix egg, lemon juice and milk and combine well.

Pour into tin 2.5 cm (1 inch) deep 25.5cm (10 inches) X 18 cm (7 inches) and bake for 1 & 1/4 hours at 325 degrees F or 160 degrees C.

Cool in tin for 15 minutes before turning out onto wire rack.

Cut into squares to serve.

Barbara was the very first person to give a recipe for this book and her delicious Ginger Raisin Cake recipe is a very handy one to have ready in case of unexpected visitors. Barbara plays an active role in church events where her baking is always very much appreciated.

lemon curd fatless sponge

Contributor: **Trish Geddes**

8 oz caster sugar

6 eggs separated

1 oz ground almonds

4 oz ground rice

grated rind and juice of 1 large lemon

icing sugar for dusting the top of cake

filling
fresh cream and lemon curd

lemon curd
3 oz caster sugar

rind and juice of 1 large lemon

2 large eggs (well beaten)

2 oz butter

Line the bases of 2 7-inch round cake tins with greaseproof paper and grease.

Separate the eggs - place yolks in the mixing bowl and add sugar and lemon juice.

Whisk mixture until thick and beginning to turn pale.

Stir in the lemon rind, ground rice and ground almonds, blending evenly.

Using a clean bowl whisk egg whites to the soft peak stage. Gently fold egg whites into lemon mixture using a metal spoon.

Divide mixture intoprepared tins and bake for 30 minutes at 180 degrees c or 160 degrees c (fan) until firm and springy in centre.

Leave to cool and fill with fresh cream and lemon curd.

Dust with icing sugar.

Lemon curd

Put sugar and lemon juice in a bowl and mix.

Add beaten eggs and put bowl over a pan of simmering water.

Add butter in small pieces.

Stir frequently until mixture thickens.

aunt mary's 'salami'

Contributor: **Agnes Nicol**

serves 4

13 digestive biscuits (crushed)

13 marshmallows (snipped)

13 cherries (chopped)

1 small tin condensed milk or enough condensed milk to bind the mixture together

coconut

Mix all ingredients together and make into one large sausage shape or two smaller ones.

Roll in coconut and put in fridge to set.

Cut into slices.

A great favourite on " Open Days!"

Agnes Nicol, Tranquillity Health and Beauty

Tranquillity Health and Beauty is a busy, well established business set in the centre of Tain High Street.

granny shivas's boiled fruit cake

Contributor: Muriel Watson

170g (6oz) currants

225g (8oz) sultanas

240ml (just under ½ pint) water

2 beaten eggs

110g (4oz) plain flour

110g (4oz) self-raising flour

110g (4oz) margarine

170g (6oz) sugar

2 level teaspoons mixed spice

1 level teaspoon baking soda

pinch salt

Preheat oven.

Place margarine, currants, sultanas, sugar, spice, bicarbonate of soda, and water in large pan and bring to boil.

Simmer for 1 minute.

Take off heat and leave to cool before adding both flours, beaten eggs and salt,

Mix really well and turn into prepared tin,

Bake at 180°C (350°F) - Gas Mark 4 - for 90 minutes approx.

Check after 75 minutes with skewer to see if cooked.

Leave to cool completely before putting in tin.

Muriel was born and brought up in Tain and returned with her husband Tony after university to buy one of the local chemists which they ran together for over 20 years. Muriel ran the local Girl Guides for much of that time and was so popular that anyone wishing to join had to be quick in putting their name down on the waiting list!

chocolate yoghurt cake

Contributor: Richard Easson

150 ml (5 fl oz) good cooking oil (sunflower)

150 ml (5 fl oz) natural yoghurt

4 level tablespoons of golden syrup

175g (6 oz) caster sugar

3 eggs

3 tablespoons cocoa

Mix all the above together and then add:-

225g (8oz) self raising flour

1/2 level teaspoon bicarbonate of soda

1/2 level teaspoon salt

Stir together and put in a lined 20cm (8 inch) lined cake tin and bake in the middle of a pre-heated oven at 170 degrees C (325 degrees F) or Gas Mark 3 for 1 & 1/2 hours.

This gives you a cake for slicing in half and filling as desired, and which can be sprinkled with icing sugar or covered in Chocolate Fudge Frosting, or icing as required by the occasion. *Richard Easson*

Richard and his wife Joan are both very talented artists. Since finishing his studies at the Edinburgh College of Art, he has exhibited regularly in group shows, and one-man shows and has also published three books of drawings Richard uses various techniques including watercolour, oil etchings, pen and ink and pencil. Having served on Tain Community Council for 12 years, Richard is very community minded and very kindly agreed to donate his beautiful pen and ink drawings for this book.

brambles carrot cake

Contributor: Christel Mercer

1 cup oil

1¾ cup brown sugar

3 eggs

3 cups coarsely grated carrots

handful of chopped walnuts

2½ cups self raising flour

½ tsp bicarbonate of soda

2tsp mixed spice

cream cheese frosting

30g (1oz) butter

80g (3oz) cream cheese, softened

1 tsp grated lemon rind

1 tbs lemon juice or vanilla essence

1½ cups icing sugar

Grease 15cm by 25cm (6" X 10") loaf pan.

Line base with greased paper. Heat oven to 160°C. (325 degrees F) Gas Mark 3.

Beat oil, sugar and eggs in a bowl with an electric mixer till thick and creamy.

Stir in carrots, nuts and sifted dry ingredients.

Pour mixture into prepared pan and bake in moderate oven for 45 minutes.

Cover loosely with foil; bake further 45 minutes. Let stand a few minutes before turning onto wire rack to cool. Top cold cake with cream cheese frosting.

Cream cheese frosting

Beat butter, cheese, rind and juice or vanilla in a small bowl with electric mixer until light and fluffy. Gradually beat in sifted icing sugar.

The recipe can be made 2 days ahead and stored in an airtight container.

Suitable for freezing.

Believed to be of American origin, carrot cakes started to become very popular in the 1950s. Although Brambles hasn't been around for that long, this is one of our most popular cakes. Our cook uses the original 'Brambles recipe' and folks return from far and wide to sample it.

Sit around a table, or linger in the soft seats and 'catch the craic' while relaxing in a welcome atmosphere at Brambles Coffee and Gift Shop. Not only can guests treat themselves to a variety of delicious home baking (cheesecakes to die for!) they can also enjoy work by local artists and wood carvings from a local craftsman that adorn the walls.

iced 'porridge' (biscuits)

Contributor: Rhoda Corsie

1¼ cups of porridge oats

¾ cup of flour

1 cup coconut

½ cup of sugar

pinch of salt

110g (4oz) margarine (melted)

Mix dry ingredients.

Pour melted margarine over.

Press into lightly greased tin.

Bake in moderate oven 190°C (375°F) - Gas Mark 5 - for 20 minutes until golden brown.

Pour 170g (6oz) of icing over porridge whilst still hot.

Allow to cool and cut into pieces

flora's flapjacks

Contributor: Flora Stone

170g (6oz) butter

110g (4oz) soft pale brown sugar

2 tablespoons golden syrup

350g (12oz) porridge oats

Melt butter, sugar and syrup.

Add porridge oats and stir well.

Spread thickly onto baking tray.

Cook in hot oven 200°C (400°F) - Gas mark 6 - for 8-10 minutes.

Flora is well known for her charity work, home baking, and coffee mornings that are always well attended You can always be sure of a cheery welcome and the above is one of the most sought after recipes friends are always asking for.

favourite recipes...

MISCELLANEOUS

ILLUSTRATION BY RICHARD EASSON

glenmorangie fizz

serves 1

Contributor: Rachel Barrie

1 champagne flute

runny honey

whisky

sparkling rose wine

finely crushed mint leaves

sugar chrystals

Take 1 champagne flute and add 1 or 1 & 1/2 measures of Glenmorangie Port Wood Finish to taste.

Drop 1/2 teaspoon of runny honey into the whisky and stir gently for 5-10 seconds - to blend in - not dissolve. The honey should settle on the bottom.

Drop 1/2 teaspoon sugar crystals into the whisky. Do not stir.

Pour in chilled sparkling rose wine to fill the flute. Garnish on top with finely crushed mint leaves.

This lovely cocktail was created by Glenmorangie's master blender Rachel Barrie.

'The key ingredient in any malt whisky is the water that goes into it. In Glenmorangie's case this comes from the Tarlogie Springs, which rise about a mile above the distillery. These waters once fell as rain on the Hill of Tain, then filtered down through lime and sandstone rocks, gathering minerals on the way, before rising again at Tarlogie. It can take up to 100 years for the falling water to emerge as spring water. So precious is this source of water that Glenmorangie has acquired the entire catchment area of the spring! '

farmhouse lemonade

makes about 16 glasses

Contributor: Paul Moclair

8 large lemons

8 oz caster sugar

4 pints of boiling water

Wash & dry lemons.

Peel of lemon peel very thinly with potato peeler or grater.

Squeeze juice from lemons and put in covered container in fridge.

Mix peel with sugar in large bowl.

Pour over boiling water, stirring briskly, cover and leave overnight in cool place.

Next day, add reserved lemon juice.

Strain into jugs and chill, consume.

elderflower champagne

Contributor: Susan Harding-Newman

(makes about 4½ litres (1 to 1¼ gallons)

6 heads of freshly picked Elderflowers in full bloom

4 litres (1 gallon) cold water

750gm (1 to 1½ lbs) sugar

2 tablespoons white wine vinegar

juice & rind of 1 lemon

Squeeze juice of lemon and put with rind and the elderflowers into a large basin.

Add sugar and vinegar.

Pour over cold water and stir well until sugar dissolves

Cover and leave to steep in a cool place for 24 hrs

Strain off and bottle in screw-topped bottles.

Leave for 2-3 months. (If you can't resist it may be drunk after 3 weeks)

'It foams delightfully when poured'

Susie is a Carnegie, brought up in the farthest NE corner of Aberdeenshire in the years after World War II when rationing was still in force but where local fresh food was always available. Having married into the military, she has lived in Europe and the United States, where she collected new ideas which influences her cooking and now lives in Ross-shire.

lassic sweet & sour yoghurt

serves 1

Contributor: Paul Moclair

½ pint of plain yoghurt

freshly ground black pepper (for sour lassie)

½ pint of cold wataer

two teaspoons of sugar (for sweet lassie)

½ teaspoon of salt

Mix all ingredients together.

Chill.

Drink.

date & apple chutney (uncooked)

Contributor: Carole Herd

1lb dates, chopped

1lb onions, chopped

1lb apples, chopped

1lb demerara sugar

½ pint brown malt vinegar

2 level teaspoons ground nutmeg

2 level teaspoons salt

2 level teaspoons made mustard

shake of pepper

Mix all the ingredients together in a big bowl and marinate for 2-3 days. Stir and put into pots.

My mother made vast quantities of this chutney - just so that she could give it away!

plum chutney

Makes approx 2.75 Kg (6lb)

Contributor: Prue Douglas Menzies

1.5Kg (3lb) stoned plums

475ml (¾ pint) vinegar

81 g (3oz) salt

27g (1oz) garlic

54g (2oz) onions

54g (2oz) sweet almonds (blanched)

900g (2lbs) sugar

250g (8oz) crystallized ginger

¼ teaspoon cayenne pepper

454g (1lb) raisins

Weigh plums after stoning.

Boil until tender in vinegar.

Stand aside to cool (closely covered)

Add raisins and the rest of ingredients cut fine or minced.

Stir well and simmer for 10 minutes.

Bottle cold in screw top jars.

Contributor: Caroline Shepherd-Baron

All of these ingredients would almost certainly have been freely available in the North of Scotland in the 6th and 10th Centuries, A.D., the time of The Picts.

crushed oats (could be porridge oats or whole oats)

blaeberries (blueberries) fresh or dried

wild raspberries fresh or dried

wild brambles fresh or dried

chopped hazelnuts

dried elderflower petals and/or berries

heather honey (from wild bees)

Mix all ingredients together with a wooden spurtle (wooden stirring stick, traditionally Scottish) in any desired quantities.

Pat into shape on a girdle or flat stone.

Divide into bannocks as required.

Caroline Shepherd Baron was responsible for a lot of the hard work that went into bringing the Tarbat Discovery Centre up to the stage where it could be opened to the public.

Tarbat Archaeological Discovery Centre is housed inside the beautifully restored 18th century Tarbat Old Parish Church, in the seaside village of Portmahomack. It was opened in 1999 by His Royal Highness, Prince Charles and is now accepted as being in partnership with The National Museums of Scotland. It has often been described as "A Jewel in the Crown of Scotland" and displays, as well, as much of the more recent history of the local area, many of the fascinating results of the archaeological excavations still being carried out on the site adjacent to the building. These have revealed segments of the site of a Pictish monastic settlement, dating back a far as the end of the 6th century AD. This is then thought to have been almost completely destroyed by Viking raiders at some time during the 10th or 11th centuries. For those interested in the history of Scotland and the lives of the people who lived there in those far-off days, a visit to this Centre is not to be missed!

martin's favourite easy breakfast

Contributor: Martin Watssman

assemble the tools of the trade !

a standard 2 egg microwave omelette maker

an egg whisk (or a fork if you don't have access to a whisk)

a jug or bowl to whisk the egg in

a microwaveable plate

a microwaveable plate cover
(not essential but it prevents spattering)

a toaster or grill (for the toast)

knife & fork (you may have to use two knives or wash one if you prefer)

assemble the ingredients !

2 eggs

a dash of milk or water

olive oil to wipe onto omelette maker if required – mine doesn't need grease

fresh basil - a little bit and finely chopped

about 60 – 100 grams of smoked salmon - enough to cover the omelette maker

tomato

lemon juice

black pepper to taste

2 slices of brown bread toast

Whisk the eggs with the dash of milk or water in the jug/bowl until airy and light.

Add a little chopped fresh basil to the mix (but not if your going to have coffee with it!)

Separate out your slices of salmon – you will need enough to line both sides of the omelette maker (but don't put it in the omelette maker yet).

Pour the mixture into the two halves of the omelette maker and cook as per instructions for your particular maker (mine is one minute then stir and then 40 seconds – yours may be different).

While this is cooking pop your toast in the toaster and let it do its thing.

When the toast pops (or you remember its under the grill before it chars completely) you can butter or low cal spread it lightly and slice into artistic triangular shapes.

Now close over the omelette maker and then open it so that one side is empty.

Line this section with smoked salmon.

Flip it closed and open it again the other way so that you can line the other side.

Now close it all over and microwave for about one and a half minutes or until salmon is well cooked. I usually turn the whole thing over half way (salmon should be opaque and pink).

Slice tomato into wedges and arrange with toast on a plate leaving space for your omelette.

You may wish to sit the omelette on a thin slice of the toast with a fresh lettuce leaf if you feel really artistic or even use bit of salad cress on top. Drizzle with lemon juice and a good screw of fresh ground black pepper.

Note that I don't add salt as the smoked salmon has enough salt for me but you may wish to season it differently. Microwaves have different powers and mine is a Class D (700 – 750W) so timings are for that machine. Also the basil and coffee thing ? Well I saw this thing about taste buds and apparently basil and coffee is a really bad combination chemically but if you want to try – go ahead. Sounds complicated but its really dead simple – enjoy !

Martin Watssman is at home storytelling and hosting workshops with primary, secondary and adult audiences. He often tests out new tales on his four children, who are his sternest critics! In the past he has been an occasional talk show presenter and voice-over artist with a local radio company. Cruise ship passengers embarking at Invergordon have a treat in store when Martin is the courier waiting to take them on their sightseeing trip. Having a busy schedule and being a crucial part of Taste of Tain events means that Martin has to be booked well in advance!

ankerville house nursery baby unit porridge

Contributor: Carol MacRae

Porridge Recipe and Procedure

(you need 4 children complete with their own bowls and wooden spoons).

ensure all hands are washed and aprons donned

help each child to measure out ½ cup of oatmeal and 2 to 2½ cups of water.

Allow them to mix the ingredients together.

Ask the children to spoon the porridge mixture into a large pot.

An adult then brings the porridge to the boil in a pot on the cooker hob.

Once the porridge has reached boiling point the temperature of the hob should be reduced to allow it to simmer for 3 minutes.

Allow the porridge to cool slightly before serving.

Milk may be poured over the porridge in bowls before eating.

Ensure the children know it holds a special ingredient so that they have a taste to try and decide what it may be.

Carol MacRae, Ankerville House Nursery/Baby Unit, Tain.

children's mayonnaise

Contributor: Irene Dewing

1 egg

1 tin condensed milk

same measure olive oil or mixture of olive oil and vegetable oil

same measure wine vinegar

1 teaspoon dried mustard powder

black pepper to taste.

Whiz all the ingredients in mixer.

Pour into screw top jar and put in the fridge.

If mixture separates give jar a good shake.

Keeps for ages!

'This recipe was found on the back of a receipt sent in a parcel from Canada to my mother-in-law during the war and is loved by everyone!' *Irene Dewing*

bacon~banana bombshells

serves 4   *Contributor:* **Mike Taylor**

4 large ripe but firm bananas.

50g (2oz) of seedless raisins.

8 rashers of rindless streaky bacon (smoked rashers are best if cooking outdoors!)

4 medium sized tomatoes

lemon juice

fine cut marmalade

olive oil

1 carton of chilled Greek yoghurt

freshly ground sea salt

freshly ground black pepper

1 large glass of port

finely chopped basil, thyme and parsley; alternatively, dried mixed herbs.

Peel the bananas, then laying them flat, scoop out the centres with a small spoon (rather iike a dugout canoe).

Using a pastry brush, brush the bananas all over with lemon juice to prevent them discolouring.

Using a small knife, spread the hollowed-out centres of the bananas thinly with marmalade.

Then chop the raisins up and use these to fill the centres completely.

Wrap the bacon rashers on a flat surface and 'spread' each one with the back of a knife until they're half as long again.

Wrap the rashers of bacon round the bananas in a spiral (two rashers should easily cover one banana) so that the bananas are completely wrapped in bacon. Cut the tomatoes in half with a 'zig- zag' cut. (to make them more decorative)

Sprinkle the halves with a little mixed herbs and olive oil.

If cooking indoors, place the wrapped bananas and tomatoes in an oven-proof dish brushed with olive oil.

Cook in a hot oven 220°C (425°F) - Gas mark 7 - for 20-25 minutes.

Alternatively, wrap the individual bananas loosely in foil; foil-wrap the tomatoes separately and cook them all over a hot barbecue for 20 minutes, or place in the hot embers of a bonfire for 25-30 minutes.

Serve each banana with two halves of tomato sprinkled (to taste) with freshly ground sea salt and black pepper.

Place a small teaspoonful of chilled yoghurt on the banana before each bite.

Oh yes...the large glass of port...Well, you sip that between mouthfuls! An' if that doesn 't convince you life's worth living...I don't know what will!

A good starter, a snack or a supper dish, but definitely best cooked on a well-established barbecue or in the ashes of a bonfire.
(Serves 4 unless like me the open air and bonfires gives you a huge appetite, in which case serves 2!)

Mike Taylor (one of Tain's hidden treasures!)

"Up on holiday are you?" Locals still ask me that. I've lived in Tain thirteen years now but I don't blame them. Illustrating as a profession is one of the least sociable careers you can choose. I see daylight as a luxury, and if the world came to an end, I'm certain I'd be the last to know. I do feel a bit isolated at times, but a good collection of videos and the odd bottle of wine helps. I've got very few responsibilities, I can wear odd socks, eat whatever takes my fancy (like peanut butter and scrambled eggs on toast1.), sit around all day watching old films while I work in a dressing gown, and I can have breakfast at 9.00pm. if I feel like it'. On the other hand, if you want a healthy income don't take up illustrating!

ACKNOWLEDGEMENTS

I'd like to take this opportunity to thank all those who made this book possible, especially the contributors who selflessly revealed for public appreciation their personal favourite recipes. Many are close friends and acquaintances that I have known for a great number of years. I would also like to express my gratitude to Melissa Gray of Grayscotland Ltd for the excellent design layout of the pages and Fiona Robertson for all her valuable help and advice. Finally I would like to thank Richard Eason, Lucy Ballantyne and Mike Taylor for their wonderfully drawn illustrations, my husband Mike for his support and photographs, freely given for use in this book, and of course to Alasdair Rhind for his vision and support.

Carole Herd